In Praise of

Written on Occasion of . . .

The insightful giftedness of the author demonstrates his depth of wisdom in the ordinary experiences of life to which the reader can easily identify.

Mrs. Connie Johnson
MDiv with Biblical Women's Studies

Tom Nordstrom's poems spell out reflection, refreshment, and relaxation. I feel like I am right there at the moment the poem is being described.

Klaris Petersen

Thomas Alan Nordstrom is the man I proudly call my dad. A Vietnam vet and cancer survivor, he weaves emotion into his poems motivated by his love for God, for family, and for life's precious moments. Nothing is more important to Dad than strong family ties. Marrying Mom and having a family of his own was something he dreamed of while serving in Vietnam. Five grandchildren are now the apple of his eye. He is the baby rocker, lullaby singer, and storyteller extraordinaire. We all praise him for his sacrificial love and generosity. He exemplifies how to serve God by loving others. With Dad, there are no strangers, only friends he has not met. My life is rich and full because of the closeness we share. Thank you, Dad, for being an amazing father and for pointing me to my heavenly Father. Thank you for loving Mom, Jon, and me without restraint and for creating a family bond that surpasses the miles between us.

Karen Russell, CPA
Proud daughter

Refreshes the heart with winsome guidance. I feel God has chosen Tom as his instrument and allowed him to witness in this way. After reviewing several of his poems, my faith tells me he will use this book to bring honor to His name.

Mrs. Jewell F. Smith
Editor
Voice of Victory Ministries

Helps believers stop seeing conflict as obstacles and start seeing them as "opportunities to glorify God." People in the most affluent societies are feeling the sense of despair and hopelessness. Hope is the medicine that can cure nearly anything. The dream never dies, only the dreamer; the song never stops, just the singer. Tom believes this: don't feel insignificant—ever!

Bloom where you are planted. Defy the troubling reports. Stay the course. Straight-ahead. Don't ever quit. Above all, keep hope alive, endure hardships—if necessary, for the most important cause in the world—seek to save that which is lost!

To know Tom is to love Tom. His poetry reflects his heart. In some way, we all share in his life experiences. Tom is a modern-day, twenty-first-century Barnabas. Encouragement is not his game, it's Tom himself.

Pastor Don
Crossroads Christian Church

Written on Occasion of . . .

Thomas A. Nordstrom

Library of Congress Control Number:		2009903781
ISBN:	Hardcover	978-1-4415-2945-9
	Softcover	978-1-4415-2944-2

This book was printed in the United States of America.

To order additional copies of this book, contact:
Xlibris Corporation
1-888-795-4274
www.Xlibris.com
Orders@Xlibris.com
56918

For my Savior and Lord Jesus Christ, my charming wife Bobbi, son Jonathan and wife Korie and daughter Karen and husband Jordan. I also include my five angels, Logan, Taryl, Lauren, Jackson Thomas, and Kaitlyn. Finally, my best friend, Don Smith and wife Jewell. Thank you for your encouragement, love and support.

Prologue
Written on Occasion of . . .

Join me in celebrating relationships with family and friends. Meditate with me on nature's beauty. Cherish and honor our country and those who gave the ultimate sacrifice to give us freedom and liberty. Appreciate God's wisdom and life's lessons in verses about faith and church.

Engage your minds in what I call a "word snapshot." Let your heart enter into both real and imaginary thoughts and ideas which I've attempted to capture through life's adventures. Many times we have an experience we can't quite put into words . . . this is the basis for my book of poems.

The names of my grandchildren, children and friends are inserted in poems, yet these events and opportunities are a part of any loving family. You'll enjoy the times with me as I describe moments of joy and growth in my angels' lives. It is amazing how children will say things that are excitingly profound. They ask very difficult questions sometimes. The answers to their questions are followed with an "I don't know, but God does", and He will tell us. A big hug and ruffle of the hair goes a long way to helping answer pop quizzes given by our grandchildren. God knows the answers, and using scripture is a solid base to answer questions such as "why?" and "how come?". Our little Taryl loves the song "Jesus Loves the Little Children," and in my poems, I attempt to find ways to show a deep thankfulness for all that God has done for us.

I have two poems about my precious mom and dad. Their love and sacrifice gave me a chance to be the first college graduate of the family tree. Neither mom nor dad finished high school, but they were very brilliant in many ways. They survived the Depression and cold winters of Minnesota. God knows I wanted to do more for them, but I was a poor schoolteacher. The day before Bobbi and I got married, I remember Dad saying that we always had a lot of love in our family. I cherish that love and have reflected on it many times for strength.

My poems are a product of being raised in a Christian home and knowing the warmth of God and firewood all these years. To this day, I love standing in front of a woodstove with a cup of java and smelling the bacon and eggs cooking on the kitchen stove. The grandeur of the Northwest with its lumber mills and timber cutting fill my mind. I loved thinking I was a young lumberjack at the age of seven.

Walk with me as I reflect on the powerful love of country of those men and women who gave their lives and now lay beneath a cold stone marker. When you read the poems about flag and country, just know that this Vietnam veteran owes a debt of love to God and country for getting me home alive. My prayer in Vietnam was that I could get home without injury, and then I would do all I could to minister encouragement to young people—and to those on my life's path. I'm the guy that will have the tears rolling first anytime "The Star-Spangled Banner" is played. It's overwhelming to remember I was in a life and death pattern for one year, and that I witnessed the death of several of my buddies. I believe that those who were Christians are now in heaven waiting for me. I want to show honor to all that gave the ultimate sacrifice by living out my life for God and country. It is my prayer that the emotion of gratitude comes through my poetry. Our country has given much to the whole world and much has been given to us. My poems attempt to reflect the joy of living under this umbrella of peace and happiness.

When I began college in San Francisco, I worked nights for UPS and tried to go to school during the day. In 1966, I dropped into part-time-student status after I couldn't keep up the full-time pace. That is exactly why I was chosen to be a part of the armed forces. Here is what I say about being drafted. Uncle Sam opened the window of opportunity, and I felt the draft. In a sense, I am still coming home from Vietnam.

I had been plucked from a struggling student's life and, in six months, was in Vietnam. Days later, I saw death firsthand and wondered if I would ever get home. The combat I was in and the loss of comrades forever changed me. My life was put on fast-forward, and I grew up too fast. I am still trying to slow life down in order that I may get a good look at it and enjoy its many dynamic twists and turns. I now count each heartbeat, breath, and moment as a gift from God.

I met Thomas Kinkade one day and want to thank him for inspiring me to be a "word" painter. Please allow yourself to journey into my poems and participate in the experiences. Thank you for experiencing life as I see it when you read my poems. God bless!

Thomas A. Nordstrom

CONTENTS

Family

Friends

Church

Nature

Patriotism

Faith

Lessons

Family

Kaitlyn

Praying for you, little girl
Your arrival will be a whirl

Questions and wonderings will abound
When asleep, no one makes a sound

Mommie's tender touch will calm
Daddies strong arms will be balm

We love you from your nose to toes
In our hearts, you are a sparkling rose

Your cheeks show hues of pink rose
Where is my camera for that cute pose?

Daddy holds you, and he is so proud
Your little cry is not very loud

The news of your arrival thrilled all
Mommie, how long before we go to mall?

I would like to tell you how it is here
All my needs come first, is that clear?

My entourage will be at least four
When I need something, you will adore

I don't like to be fed late—be on time
I like a variety of food—hold the lime

When I sleep, I want total quiet
Any disturbance may affect my diet

If I ever scream, come running to me
What I want I want now, don't you see?

I am the third child—loved you from start
I love you, Mom and Dad, here's my heart

~   ~   ~   ~   ~   ~   ~   ~   ~   ~   ~

Written on occasion of holding little Kaitlyn for the first time. She stole my heart, and I think she liked me rocking her and singing my homespun songs. I see her every day now, but only in my mind and photos. Our family ties are so strong, and as Kaitlyn grows up, I want to see her experiencing all the discoveries of this wonderful world and of Jesus as her Savior. Bless you, little angel, and thanks for loving me. From the Grandpa that tends to get misty eyed because he is so blessed.

~   ~   ~   ~   ~   ~   ~   ~   ~   ~   ~

J.T., My Pal

J.T., my pal, goes by J.T. to family and friends
You will see him hold a toy needing mends

He is two years old and steals hearts
Soon he'll want to push grocery carts

An analyzer-mechanic loves wheels that spin
He searches and finds a certain toy in the bin

He rides his fire truck fast and then turns
The world is his classroom, and he learns

He and sister Taryl really race along
Their home is always humming with a song

J.T. loves to snuggle up and look at a book
When he is happy, you can tell by his look

J.T. really, really loves helicopters all whirly
His imagination sees helicopters as twirly

Construction toys really put him in a zone
He'll never ever turn down an ice cream cone

J.T., the maestro, walks up to the piano and plays
Variety—food—sleep fill his young days

J.T., you are now two years old and doing so much
Secure in Dad's strength and mom's loving touch

The future is brand new, wish I could take a peek
I'd see you—special and precious and unique

You are a celebrity with a full heart of love
You're the pied piper with peace and a dove

It's great to be together and experience life
When we play our games, I lose much of strife

Happy birthday, J.T.—hearts beat strong for you
We all love you, and Jesus loves you too.

~   ~   ~   ~   ~   ~   ~   ~   ~   ~   ~

Written on occasion of J.T.'s second birthday. What a joyous occasion for all
that attend. Take a picture fast because he is growing up fast. He and I are so
close. I always want to be a grandpa he can be really proud of. I remember
the first time I saw you, big boy, and a poem I had written before you were
born came alive. It goes like this:

It was a January cold, clear day
When Jackson Thomas came our way
When I looked into his precious little face
I learned more of God's amazing grace

Take good care of your middle name. I am honored that you are named after
me. We leave this scene with both parents beaming, and everyone chatting.
There is more than enough food for all, and the cake is mandatory. J.T. is
now opening gifts and doesn't take long to rip the wrapping. Later after his
nap, J.T. and Dad go to the hardware store because J.T. really loves it and
really loves his dad. Before bedtime, J.T. puts both hands on Mom's face
and draws her down for a special kiss.

~   ~   ~   ~   ~   ~   ~   ~   ~   ~   ~

Pop

A three-letter word that evokes a lot
My pop was a man who the Lord sought

The Lord and pop found each other, yes
Pop from that day gave others a bless

His love for me was strong and true
A true friend and others to him drew

Hard working and dedicated to his job
He provided well—even corn on cob

He sang solos in church—from heart
His love for Mom would never part

He and I worked and played together
We walked life's path on rock or heather

Pop taught me a lot, and I reflect on him
The memories of Pop will never dim

He gave me secure love and adventure
I remember when Pop got his denture

I learned how to love God and others
Pop was a true servant with no covers

Pop was always proud of me, I know
I loved and respected him, did it show?

I was six months old when I squeezed his hand
Home from the war—his kisses did land

On his deathbed, I tried to understand
Last thing I did was to hold his hand

He now was free of pain and with the Lord
He was my strong warrior with his sword

I looked at him with tears that blurred me
Pop, you were special and precious, you see

I'll see my pop again in heaven someday
I want to be like him, oh Lord, this I pray

My pop was my hero and not just in name
His heart was an altar and you, Lord, the flame

~ ~ ~ ~ ~ ~ ~ ~ ~ ~ ~

Written on occasion of thinking about my pop who I loved with all my heart. I saw him give sacrificially and put others first. I saw him tie his boots and head for work in all kinds of weather. His Lord and his family were his thrill. I really wish he was here to help me row my boat, and then I wouldn't have this lump in my throat. Thanks, Pop, and until we see each other again, you will always be a special source of happy memories and skills learned. I miss you, Dad, so much that I feel like bawling my eyes out. You would understand. Thanks, Dad.

~ ~ ~ ~ ~ ~ ~ ~ ~ ~ ~

Mother Dearest

How did you do it mom? Five kids
All those jars you canned with lids

That sewing and mending late at night
A true picture of industry under light

Your unconditional love was so secure
You gave everything for me, Mom dear

Laundry and dishes and so much more
You never stopped—always at chore

You sang God's praises as you worked
Victory was yours—even as enemy lurked

From school, you were oft at the door
Be a worker, not a schirker—do more

That was your theme, and you lived it
The harsh winters, you gave a mitt

Homemade bread, cookies, and cake
Took much energy to bake and bake

Was your reward in our grin on chin
There was no joy in muddy boots—in

You lived through the Depression years
Memories of cherished friends brought tears

Thanks for being there for me—fit or ill
I made trouble, but you loved me still

Remember we laughed and laughed out loud
Through the trials, you carried no cloud

Your faith was so strong and courage too
When with you, one could never be blue

When you were dying, some of me died too
Mother, I loved you through and through

Mom, I'll never forget your last breath
Jesus took your soul—victory in death

Mother dearest, I still love you very much
You were loving and kind—had a godly touch

Everything you taught me and things you said
Will be cherished and so fresh in my head

Mom, I wish I could have done more for you dear
You are special and precious and always near

I have cried so many times that you loved me
Thankful for a Hall of Famer mom, you see

Memories of you will not ever be weak or part
Because Mom, I hold you in the center of my heart

⌐ ⌐ ⌐ ⌐ ⌐ ⌐ ⌐ ⌐ ⌐ ⌐ ⌐

Written on occasion of remembering the avalanche of things that Mom and
I did together over the years. (She did not even have running water in the
early years but managed to carry on in spite of several hardships. Having the
war took Dad away for months.) Mom was a picture of an energizer rabbit.
Her godly love shown in her beautiful dark brown eyes. Her life formula was
to put herself last. Your love gave me strength and still does today. When I
see you in heaven, I'll say thanks.

Mother dearest, for all you did for me and for believing in me—Mom, I
love you—let it echo through all heaven, Mom what was that remedy you
had for treating a really big lump in your throat?

⌐ ⌐ ⌐ ⌐ ⌐ ⌐ ⌐ ⌐ ⌐ ⌐ ⌐

Return of a Hero

I launched out on my own
Worked hard seeds sown

Heading home in just a few hours
Flying over mountains and towers

Can't wait to see, my loved
Peace in heart has been doved

Listen to the unborn pulse
This is real and never false

Familiarity around me, yes, retort
Pressure and pleasure in a sort

Being home seems surreal
Wife and son are a big deal

Jet lag and mind of events
Don't let things make me tense

Things to do and will it be done
Let's start with the laundry spun

Loose ends tied, oh boy, yes
Business grows with no jes

A hero now has landed
Little family around him banded

My wife loves me with full heart
From her love, I'll never depart

Flowers, pictures, and home pies
Son loves me—it's in his eyes

Tired now—sleep I am craving
Holy Spirit gives me laving

Bird's-eye view shows peace
Lord, douse me and never cease

I'm really home—no more doubt
Fear is gone and no more bout

Let's go for walk or a ride
Stay real close by my side

Written on occasion of Logan and Korie welcoming home their hero Jonathan. And he is so happy. Strong family and strong love.

Hey—Wait for Me

This hospital I'm in is very busy
I lay here connected—and dizzy

Wait for me—I'm here for now
Somehow, I got here—but how?

Look at me—I'm in lots of pain
When it's over—it's all sweet gain

Mom and Dad have given so much
They give me strength—love touch

Wait for me—I'm trying to get better
At interludes, my diaper gets wetter

Wait for me and please have a heart
Don't go ahead and leave me at start

Sometimes my eyes are filled with tears
Good thing I don't know much about fears

Sometimes I am a very happy little boy
My eyes are clear and filled with joy

My heart is helping me grow bit by bit
Excuse me, please—morphine will hit

Look away as I grimace in pain
Can you see me through the stain?

Wait, please—I am a very eager kid
Soon tubes and needles I'll be rid

Another one—still, I am to lay
Makes me cry—what is an x-ray?

Don't be in a hurry, I have a dream
Dad and I are pals eating ice cream

Look at me, I'm pushing a barrel
Hey, wait for me, big sister Taryl

A woman says, "Would you like another?"
With all my heart, I love you, Mother

We four are again together and true
It was really hard on you and me too

Morphine made me—my face—to scratch
In the way was that old oxygen tube patch

Hey, wait for me, I won't quit or stray
First, though I'm overwhelmed—let's pray

Thanks, Lord, for this trial, I'm blessed
You knew everything but—well—I guessed

When we get home, a request in my head
Can we all four cuddle in your big, big bed?

After we are all done cuddling in that space
Can I watch my program—the happy fireplace?

Don't worry bout me—come in or go about
My favorite thing to do is just to hang out

As the fireplace sends its light all aglow
I want my life story with Jesus to show

⁓ ⁓ ⁓ ⁓ ⁓ ⁓ ⁓ ⁓ ⁓ ⁓ ⁓

Written on occasion of being with Jackson Thomas Russell at Easter time and having him near and not in the hospital. What a heartfelt time is had by any/all who are there—a time to celebrate the goodness of God. We look in for a moment and see folks getting ready to leave for home. Pictures are taken, and Karen and Jordan have never looked happier. Taryl is dancing and singing "You Are My Sunshine." J.T. has fallen asleep and is being called angelic by all. Grandma Bobbi says to Karen and Jordan that she has prayed for their strength several times a day. Granny's pilgrim's rest apartment has served everyone well, and as we depart from this scene, we can be assured of two things: (1) everyone thanks the Lord, (2) everyone needs some rest. Mom, you can ride with us and sit with J.T. and Taryl, if Dad doesn't mind. We'll need to stop at your place anyway. Little man, are you waking up? Jordy, I need to nurse J.T. before we leave. Granny offers another round of tea and cookies. Grandpa and Taryl play piano and sing "You Are My Sunshine."

Precious Lil' Pal

Not quite three but ideas plus
We talked and did art without fuss

Just before bedtime and bath too
Grandpa and Taryl—grapes not blue

Hide and seek through finger masks
No stress here on heavy tasks

Playing games and passing quietness
What a little angel and soft caress

No batteries or Tevo buttons to push
So quiet together enjoying the hush

Little hands drawing with crayons bright
Ole Grandpa will always remember tonight

We sang songs and loved rhythm band
Everything we did seemed so very grand

Sat by her filled with amazement and joy
Here she is, and we thought she'd be a boy

These two hours pass too fast for me
I enjoy doing things that are almost three

I pledge to you, lil' pal, that I'll do my all
To help you in life, walk and not crawl

Your eyes, my drawings have glanced
Your grandpa says you are advanced

Our togetherness makes my heart good
I'd see you every day if I could—I would

It is later in the evening—lights are dim
Ole grandpa's joy is filled to the brim

You are asleep now, my own lil' girl
On your neck, hair lies in perfect curl

I love it when you say, "My do, my do"
Mr. Right will someday hear your "I do"

Until then and after, big sister to be
God soon blesses you with bro J.T.

Thank you, Lord, for the Russells four
I thoroughly love them to the core

~   ~   ~   ~   ~   ~   ~   ~   ~   ~   ~

Written on occasion of babysitting Taryl for two hours while Mom and Grandma went Christmas shopping. Next time she comes over, I'll show her the drawings we did, and she can tell me all about them. Thanks, Lord, for the little pal you gave to me.

~   ~   ~   ~   ~   ~   ~   ~   ~   ~   ~

The Living Poem

It was a January cold, clear day
When Jackson Thomas came our way

When I looked into his precious little face
I learned more of God's amazing grace

~ ~ ~ ~ ~ ~ ~ ~ ~ ~ ~

Written on occasion of seeing Jackson Thomas for the first time. It was an honorable moment, and his condition was much better than expected. Tomorrow, he'll have the challenge of blood-flow changes, and we'll know more tomorrow evening. Thank you, Lord, for all the people praying and for every perfect provision.

To God be the glory. Great things he has done.

~ ~ ~ ~ ~ ~ ~ ~ ~ ~ ~

Push the Button

The phone revealed her voice
What a joy—caused a rejoice

She talked of her books and dresses
Did she know my melting of stresses?

Happy times thrilled my heart
Too bad we were far apart

No matter how busy I am
I always want to talk to my lamb

She says I miss you—I get sad
When I see you again, oh glad

Tell me if you remember our walk
There were so many wonders to talk

Special and precious, yes, you are
Joy together whether in home or car

Push the button, Grandpa has to go
Head says go, but heart says no-no

You push the button, easier for me
We'll talk again very soon, you'll see

Love you too, my heart stands tall
Button clicks, and heart takes a fall

⌐ ⌐ ⌐ ⌐ ⌐ ⌐ ⌐ ⌐ ⌐ ⌐ ⌐ ⌐

Written on occasion of thinking about my habit of letting my little loved
ones push the button to end our conversation. For some reason, it is easier
for me than me ending our chat. I listen for the disconnect sound and then

take a sigh of joy and carry on with my day, realizing that I've just been given a dose of powerful love that has my heart so full and overflowing. We leave this scene with Grandpa walking to the kitchen for a snack and bragging to Grandma how wonderful our little angels are. Send and End are only one-letter different, but I want to push the Send instead of the End.

⌒   ⌒   ⌒   ⌒   ⌒   ⌒   ⌒   ⌒   ⌒   ⌒   ⌒

Little Pink Sandal

Where did it come from, lying over there?
Why was there just one and not a pair?

A very young girl's summertime wear
Caused me to stop and just stare

My three granddaughters have same
Whose shoe, and what is her name?

It'll lie there until kicked aside
My happy thoughts, I cannot hide

I think of my three babes girling and twirling
They smile brightly, and hair is curling

This little sandal there for a reason
My little three darlings are in my season

I pray for them and love their joy
Nothing they do will ever annoy

Little pink sandal, you make me think
From Grandpa's duties I'll never shrink

Sandal, you remind me of all those toes
How much I miss them, only God knows

Running feet, walking feet, joyous feet
Trying to remember all is no feat

My favorite kind is the running feet
A little one running to me to again meet

Little pink sandal, who walked in you?
How old is she now, is she happy or blue?

So many shoes get left aside and behind
This little pink sandal brings joy to mind

～ ～ ～ ～ ～ ～ ～ ～ ～ ～ ～

Written on occasion of seeing this little pink sandal near my work truck lying in the gravel. We had just returned from seeing two of our three little angel girls, and I was still really missing them. Thank God, the third little angel lives close by. You know those summertimes when it seems that the little ones are all wound up and really enjoying playing outside. Everyone is laughing and talking, and burgers are on the grill. Maybe grandpas have a part in making their gals feel love, honored, and cherished; and maybe granddaughters will someday remember what genuine love and fun are as they select the man they want to marry. Grandpa and Grandma, want you to remember that we only married once.

～ ～ ～ ～ ～ ～ ～ ～ ～ ～ ～

One of the Best Sisters I'll Ever Have

I found my bed
Lay down my head

Prayed for country and loved ones
I now have granddaughters and grandsons

Each day starts with an alarm bong
Oh Lord, each morn you give a new song

Fill my tank, Lord, with your peace
You know I want wars to cease

Thank you for blessings I count
I love to drink from your fount

Good night, Lord, sleepy now
Each moment of life to you, I bow

ᵔ ᵔ ᵔ ᵔ ᵔ ᵔ ᵔ ᵔ ᵔ ᵔ ᵔ

Written on occasion of prioritizing what's most important in life. I'm thinking about Connie and writing this late-nite note to tell her how very missed she is and am praying for her and the family. I am so blessed, and I just sit here in awe of all the resources and opportunities in life. Oh Lord, you have given me so very much. One thing more I request, a grateful heart.

ᵔ ᵔ ᵔ ᵔ ᵔ ᵔ ᵔ ᵔ ᵔ ᵔ ᵔ

Rose

The first rose of spring, I did pick
Lovingly yes, a thorn not to stick

Spotless rose, oh perfect in hue
Thorns protected you as you grew

Sun came over to give awe warmth
Sun, it was you that gave rose prompth

All the world should see this precious
Its brilliance abounds and is luscious

Granddaughters are coming to adore
This rose with them will really score

Darling of spring, you warm the colder
Stunning, yes, in the eyes of beholder

Everything else on table must match
Polished, folded, without a scratch

Napkins, forks, spoons all in place
You adorn gracefully—even the lace

Two granddaughters and two moms
Even a basket with colorful poms

A symphony of smells strikes chord
So joyful here—thank you, good Lord

That rose—that rose—I say, "Oh wow"
From godchild makes a soul bow

Hurried before, the door bell did ring
Wanted to have the pick of spring

Queen rose, you adorn table of mine
Quietly, you show God's glory—shine

Memorial sweet—this royal guest
Help me, Lord, to want to do my best

First fruit of my garden, I give over
Accept me—of my soul, you are lover

Your creation—always has a godly face
Today, I was touched by amazing grace

You rose—my first pick of spring
You and God have made me sing

~ ~ ~ ~ ~ ~ ~ ~ ~ ~ ~

Written on occasion of smelling the first rose of spring from Bobbi's rose garden. It quietly reminded me of the glory of God. God is perfect and wants just the very best from us. His forgiveness is perfect for me—and I am glad he paid the price for me on the cross.

Hugs and kisses and then aprons aflare—the girls do the cleanup while grandmother sits and looks at the happy scene.

~ ~ ~ ~ ~ ~ ~ ~ ~ ~ ~

Shroud or Fog

The young boy looked at the field
Fog was rising and lifting shield

Shrouding the ground all night
Lifting now with a slow might

He ran to it with arms open wide
Hoping to touch it in fast stride

With smiling face, getting all wet
Found an old stump and just set

This scene was fun and God sent
The time here was very well spent

Sun's rays were like arrows down
This veiled curtain was rising roun

He ran back for breakfast and dry
Inside, he said, "This is my, oh my"

Soon the fog would open curtain be
The world stage would be to see

Gathered up and on bus for school
Fog rises, showing lambs with wool

As a young man and fog rises now
A memory is jogged and given bow

As he grows older, huge is the stage
Different now as if running in cage

Lord, to these memories give me send
Shroud rises, and show never ends

Show is complex, and I say with sincere
The plot isn't easy and not real clear

I walk up and become part of the cast
Lord, when shroud rises, wear no mask

Don't know how it happened—I'm all ajar
I was in audience, and now I'm the star

Fog rises, scenery in place, ready to go
Steady knees because God leads show

I've learned my lines, I'll move on cue
Theater of life has a really big view

He's older now—many shows under belt
Love's to go back to feelings felt

He loves the fog and sun shining thro
Your blessings, Lord, are always new

Thanks, Lord, I stand in total awe
For the beautiful fog I see, and I saw

⌐   ⌐   ⌐   ⌐   ⌐   ⌐   ⌐   ⌐   ⌐   ⌐   ⌐

Written on occasion of thinking back when our son Jonathan and I would
observe the rising of the fog and the glorious mixture of sun and mist.
Every day brings a new show of promise and opportunity. Take me back
there once in a while, Lord, and then I can see the shroud lifting a little
clearer. Amen.

⌐   ⌐   ⌐   ⌐   ⌐   ⌐   ⌐   ⌐   ⌐   ⌐   ⌐

Car-go

It served us well—the old car must go
Strong memories well up though

Each of our newborns came home in rig
Yes, each little one now grown so big

So many hours spent behind that ole wheel
At first, it was so cool and was real deal

I looked back at my three little ones—sardined
Too small now—'twas a fact not just seemed

It'll always be in memory and pictures too
It's not a living thing, so don't sound boohoo

Someone else will love that old car-go
They will also wash and wax and make glow

Newer car is roomier and fresh and grrrreat
We are so excited. Let's drive, I can't wait

Come on, Daddy, why did you stop?
We have to open new doors and in to hop

A shop guy was driving old rig out to the back
Old memories hit me like a heavy old sack

Come on, Daddy, little hands pulled me along
After we get in and ready, can I eat my Ding Dong?

Thrilled and thankful, our old rig is now gone
Mixed feelings abide with me—right or wrong

I know every nick and cranny and each flaw
Remember that dental trip, pain in my jaw

Turned over my keys—papers all signed
Soon out of sight and out of my mind

God has blessed us with this newer rig
Sure, will make shopping a happier gig

I look at my family each strapped in seat
Having this rig is very, very super neat

That old rig helped as our family grew
We are zooming along, yes, the same crew

Did this together, this blessing we're proud
So happy that I could just sing out loud

We're finally at home, opening doors a snap
How precious, we have three taking a nap

Exhausted, we sit on couch—oven cooks roast
We click our ice tea glasses—a sincere toast

~   ~   ~   ~   ~   ~   ~   ~   ~   ~   ~

Written on occasion of thinking about Jon and Korie and kids all jazzed about their newer rig and driving down the road busily talking about the car. We leave this scene with Korie taking a nap and Jon doing things in the yard and shop and the kids are still asleep. Now it's almost time for bed, and Logan is using his trusty flashlight to shine light on the newer rig. Lauren says, "Kiss, Daddy." After Jon gives Korie one of those longer-than-usual hugs and kisses, he then kisses Lauren. Kaitlyn tries to eat yogurt with a spoon. After hugs, kisses, and prayers, everyone is soon asleep.

~   ~   ~   ~   ~   ~   ~   ~   ~   ~   ~

Dad, is This Right?

My dad works so hard both day and night
I'm painting with you, Dad, is this right?

The old shed needed paint on new boards
Good thing, we didn't use brushes as swords

Dad instructed me on the method to use
I did my best, and he didn't blow a fuse

My dad and I are such pals, you see
When it is safe, my dad includes me

He must have very good patience now
I must slow things down—and how

I love my dad so much—he loves me
When we work together, I'm so happy

Would hate it to watch him while inside
When we are done, we're going for a ride

My dad loves me, he hugs me every day
Working together, he shows the way

Shouldn't ever paint against the grain
Makes painting a chore and full of pain

I drop my brush and run off to play
Don't run from job, here to just stay

We talked and worked and had such fun
A great feeling when job was all done

Mom took picture of painters kneeling down
Wow, Dad, this is the best shed in town

I want to always be just like my awesome dad
He knows so much and teaches me, I'm glad

Written on occasion of Korie saying that Jon and Logan are out, painting on the shed. Brings back memories of Jon and I working on projects and also having fun along the way. We leave this scene with Logan running to the window and telling Korie to look at the great paint job. I helped paint it, Mom. I know honey, and I am very proud of you. Dad and son went for a special ride after lunch, and it just so happens that a special train exhibit was downtown, and it was a surprise to Logan. People that run off and play don't know how to work 'til the job is done. Isn't that right, Dad? That's right, big fella.

Bobbi Over There

She is in Virginia, I know
She makes my heart glow

So busy having family fun
She watches as loved ones run

I carry her heart all around
Ears of soul hear the sound

God bless my Bobbi over there
Her return will bring much to share

⌐ ⌐ ⌐ ⌐ ⌐ ⌐ ⌐ ⌐ ⌐ ⌐ ⌐

Written on occasion of wanting my Bobbi over there visiting Jonathan and family to have an e-mail to read and possibly to grin over.

⌐ ⌐ ⌐ ⌐ ⌐ ⌐ ⌐ ⌐ ⌐ ⌐ ⌐

Coupon Shows Safe Way

A generous, kind daughter gave her dad a coupon
The father could get a free sandwich with poupon

Her love for him was evident and really true
This free-sandwich idea was really cool

It was made exactly to his wishes and size
Eyes bigger than stomach, he began to realize

After eating the sandwich, he began to relax
A great, loving gift—free and without tax

Jesus died for my sins—a coupon for life
He will give strength for all of life's strife

Won't forget that coupon and this day
Now I'm happy I took the safe way

~ ~ ~ ~ ~ ~ ~ ~ ~ ~ ~

Written on occasion of enjoying a sandwich from Safeway that Karen, my wonderful daughter, had provided for me. My hunger level, Safeway, and that coupon all got together at the same time. Karen, you are so kind and generous and always thinking of your dad. These are big days and exciting days, and just a moment, I have a coupon here that says you are entitled to turn this coupon in for an awesome bouncing little baby grandson.

[It was a January cold, clear day
When Jackson Thomas came our way

When I looked into his precious little face
I learned more about God's amazing grace]

~ ~ ~ ~ ~ ~ ~ ~ ~ ~ ~

Wife

Wife doesn't belong at the end
She is someone heaven did send

It's always husband and then wife
She is the one to add joy to life

She is not easy to measure
This person who is an invaluable treasure

The glow of her warmth fills the room
She is busy all day with pen, pot, or broom

One day, this helpmate God did give
He said that together we would really live

Our children reflect the love you have
Your voice on phone is a wonderful salve

Me and thee, are we still becoming one?
Right from the beginning, my heart you won

My Valentine come and hold my hand
Look, two children and five that are grand

Rest in chair with baby under blanket warm
This child feels safe and secure in your charm

We are so blessed—at the last count of blessings
We can overcome all of life's pressings

Thank you for all your love and sharing
Through the years, we've made good pairing

When we first met, for me, it was love on spot
Slightly wounded from Cupid's arrow shot

May you always love me, my honey-kuns
May all your problems just be little ones

~ ~ ~ ~ ~ ~ ~ ~ ~ ~ ~

Written on occasion of thinking about my darling wife and how awesome she is. Our home is filled with love and respect, and our grandchildren feel very good here. Thank God we have such great times. You are so correct, my dear, and thank you for expending your energy to assist me in my driving of the car.

~ ~ ~ ~ ~ ~ ~ ~ ~ ~ ~

Celbiday

We set aside a day for joy
We celebrate a birthday boy

Each moment with him is treasure
His entertainment has no measure

His mobility has changed a bit
He doesn't want to just sit and sit

He screams just to sound the alarm
Trying to communicate—no harm

His eyes tell so very, very much
We love his loving, tender touch

He sometimes feels pretty blue
Another tooth is coming through

He changes often—this lil' laddy
He's home, yes, my awesome daddy

Mommie is my pal, her love cures
Her loving eyes, yes, my heart lures

We've been through a lot, I'm told
Each day a blessing as I get old

Not hard to count candles on my cake
Blow it out, but how much breath to make?

Celbiday is fun, and I laugh with you
I'm big, and I'm one—it is really true

Taryl, I love you with all my heart
Loved you my whole life from the start

My eyes are on my daddy outside
I'll learn from him—he will be a guide

Mommie, last night wasn't much sleep
Tonight, I'll last longer—not a peep

When I'm nursing and look into your eyes
Mother and child, is this called paradise?

Full of surprises—me—nothing bores
Mommie found small toys in kitchen drawers

I'm grown up, and I have needs, you see
Would the red dodge work well for me?

Anyone have a tape measure, please
My eyelashes are the longest Grandma sees

Months ago, I made a rule that is now set
Just when you go to sleep, then I wet

When you pray, you end with an amen
Who is Jesus, such reverence to bend

Do you like my party and all the noise?
It is sure—I am not starved for toys

I look like my mother and my dad
I'm their unique son—and I am glad

What's your hurry—party's just begun
Stay at least until setting of the sun

Thanks on my celbiday to take part
Thank you, Jesus, from my whole heart

~ ~ ~ ~ ~ ~ ~ ~ ~ ~ ~

Written on occasion of anticipating J.T.'s birthday party. He is our little hero for going through so much at three months old. God has been so good to us, and if you want to know more about J.T., just ask Denny and Tammy or Tom and Bobbi. These grandparents know what to say even with a tear in their eyes. Sometimes all I can say is

> It was a January cold, clear day
> When Jackson Thomas came our way
> When I looked into his precious little face
> I learned more of God's amazing grace

We leave this happy scene as little Taryl gets on Grandpa Tom's lap and asks, "Grandpa, what is amazing grace?" As he explains the best he can, others are looking out at the pond with a hot cup of drink in their hand or sitting in front of the fireplace, relaxing. Jordan and Karen are caught kissing in the pantry, and Taryl is about to present a special creative number for her brother Jackson Thomas while she is wearing her tap shoes. She is about to begin, and everyone enjoys her look of joy and love.

~ ~ ~ ~ ~ ~ ~ ~ ~ ~ ~

Grandpa, Look at the Rainbow

The sun shone through the prismed window
Look, look it's on my face and even my toe

She and I moved our hands into the beam
The colors were so bright and clean

Her discovery was joyous for both of us
I savored this time together—not in rush

At one point, the rainbow was on her face
I needed this time and God's amazing grace

The rainbow, the promise—this was so rich
I could do this full time—this is my niche

A full time of discovery and such bliss
You'll take care of her, Lord, never miss

Rainbows remind us of God's forever love
Many blessings—can't catch in a catcher's glove

God promises to always love you so much
He'll always guide you with a loving touch

See the edges of the colors, fuzzy, huh?
Why is that I say with a rah, rah, rah, rah

Look closely, and you'll see a new color
Sometimes very bright or can be duller

God mixes and blends colors for us
Or just one color like a yellow school bus

We are something like colors—bright or dull
We allow God to mix and blend us—it's his call

I pray that your life becomes a godly portrait
To be beautiful on any given date

Rainbows are promises that God colors our life
There is a color for joy and a color for strife

We learn from joy and strife—and blossom out
Say I love and praise you, Lord, with a shout

       ◠   ◠   ◠   ◠   ◠   ◠   ◠   ◠   ◠   ◠   ◠

Written on occasion of Taryl discovering the colorful light shining on the
floor of her living room—one of those cherishable memory gems. Afterward,
she said, "We could take a picture of the rainbow and make a puzzle and
then put it on the computer and see how it fits together. This Grandpa said
that that is amazing coming from a four-year-old granddaughter. We leave
this scene with everyone going out to the car. Grandma said, "Taryl, that
is good scientific thinking." Occupants are outside now, but the rainbow
colors are still shining in. Good Lord, thanks.

       ◠   ◠   ◠   ◠   ◠   ◠   ◠   ◠   ◠   ◠   ◠

Blurry

The pressure was overheating
But, my Lord, I was heeding

Focus and work hard, yes
God's guidance takes the guess

No looking back to count steps
God's wisdom from the depths

Things appear a little blurry
Not because of snow flurry

Been given the holy nod
Paramed, not paramod

Challenge comes and tests me
My strength comes from thee

Things come in a rush
Be still and know a hush

Confident, I step over the line
You and I, Lord, today will shine

~ ~ ~ ~ ~ ~ ~ ~ ~ ~ ~

Written on occasion of Jon's prep and wait time for the word on his written test results. Nothing is too hard for the Lord, and Jon is a thorough champion. He has memorized Proverbs 3:5 and 6. Promises with obedience equals triumph. God bless you, son.

~ ~ ~ ~ ~ ~ ~ ~ ~ ~ ~

Is This a Touchdown, Dad?

This game of football is tough
Sometimes life is just plain rough

I'm not full of energy right now
Pray for me that I'll know how

I have the ball, and I'm running swell
I lean on the Lord—his is a deep well

The opposition is prepared to hit hard
As I move, I am always on keen guard

I'll make you proud—just wait and see
It's early in the game—I'll be all I can be

Each step I take—I'll be very, very glad
Thinking of the hero of the game—you Dad

When you are home with me, I'll shout
It's time for Dad and I to just hang out

Each moment now—brings new things to do
We can play catch—four wheel—or use glue

Hey, Dad, is this a touchdown yet?
I'm doing a lot of waiting now, but no regret

Take my hand, Dad, prepare me for the test
Your prayer and strength—help me to rest

I hear your voice and know who you are
I feel better when you are near, not far

Love ya, Dad, for all you do for your family
Show me the shop—I want to copy your handily

The warmth of fireplace and glow it projects
Reminds me much that you and God protect

Can we do things together? Let me help, please
Helping and doing with you, Dad, gives me ease

God's in charge—come on my hero Dad—let's roll
The kickoff is scheduled soon—I'll make a goal

Written on occasion of thinking about all the fun times J.T. is going to have
with his dad, Jordan. As this great, wonderful big world unfolds before him,
J.T. will be so thankful that he has the best dad in the whole world.

No Turning Back

The world changed, and I have
No other influence than God's salve

Discipline is a very bitter pill
Thank you, taxpayers, I'll pay my bill

Soon I'll look through freedom's glass
Studied hard and passed every class

Oddly miss, this place, it's been my home
Worked my fingers to the bone

No one here wants me back
Going out that gate with no slack

Please don't look down on me
I've been forgiven, I'm set free

Looking back does one thing good
Reveals to us the could or the should

Lord, give me a purpose, peace, and sign
Praise you a lot, and at home, I'll dine

I'll take a deep breath and homeward face
Powered by you, Lord, and your amazing grace

Real joy only comes from you, Lord
I've developed a trust for your Word

When I get home and see Mom and Dad
Such deep new meaning to the word *glad*

Moving now from point A to point B
I can do it because I'm a new me

Opportunities and love are piled up in a stack
No desire for the old way of sidetrack

Moving on and can't see the gutter
That kind of life makes me shudder

God has promised to give an abundant life
He'll give strength and joy for any strife

Bloom where planted and really grow
God plucks seeds that we sow

Sins now afar from the east to the west
With you, Lord, I'll do my very, very best

Close the book and bury it deep
The new book's pages make hearts leap

～　　～　　～　　～　　～　　～　　～　　～　　～　　～　　～

Written on occasion of nephew Jeremy Nordstrom making a final push in prison school to complete everything and return home, changed and free to make correct choices after conferring with God.

～　　～　　～　　～　　～　　～　　～　　～　　～　　～　　～

Blankets

Blankets feel good—tuck in your toes
Until room is warm—cover your nose

The companion to blanket is a book
Joyous time by fireplace or in nook

Good time-out—count me in
Old model blankets may be thin

Tightly fit blanket gives a hug
Blanket falls off shoulder tug

Phone rings, and let it go
Can't move just watching the snow

Little daughter comes near and cold
Blanket calls her—she is sold

Cozy and what joy it has been
Little chick under wing of hen

My security blanket allows me rave
This warmth, I want to always save

Watching snow-under blanket, I sit
Hot tea sits there cooling a bit

Time is slow, and I enjoy my part
Lord, help me keep a grateful heart

The table holds my to-do list
For now, this I wouldn't have missed

I feel like a baby—all snug and warm
A sleeping child is filled with charm

Snow enters stage—slow and steady
I love snow, and I am always ready

I can watch the snow or be in it
Crunching under boot or held in mitt

Heavy and thick, the branches bow
No braking or snapping but how

Scene so beautiful, boot prints will mar
No driving today snow heavy on car

Inside, one covers me outside, one to view
I cuddle inside while outside is white and new

Little angel's first winter of snow
Learning God's blessings, I know

Waiting for snow or remember it past
Next day, it can sure melt fast

Stray bird comes, and voice is mute
When it leaves to take a southern route

Everything is cold, quiet, and bright
So glad I can really share this sight

If the snow melted now, then sorrow
We'll wait to enjoy it tomorrow

Camera tries to portray this art
Remembered through eye and heart

Visitors trudge to door at ten
I postpone my writing, lay down pen

These friends are really happy to see
This snowy masterpiece given to me

Colors and hews and just right sizes
When awarded gets all the top prizes

Paint and brush try to save it
No competition—God gave this hit

This snow and home, a living play
I write in journal without delay

Next in this play is a hot meal
Vegetables and spice and a little veal

Desserts now start in mouth to melt
We forget frozen feet how they felt

This is our castle—down there is some moat
We slide on to bag and then again tote

Bedtime now, and I'll sleep well, you'll see
Bed is soft, and my blanket gives glee

Ours are out, but God's light comes soon
It reflects on the snow from the moon

Thanks for the blankets, I am sincere
Every day your love is true and clear

Written on occasion of Karen and Taryl waiting for Jordan to return to help
them enjoy the beautiful snow blanket.

Too Two

Happy second birthday, Taryl sweet
You are special to me and that's neat

Your arrival was special in so many ways
Prince not princess was the Russell craze

I prayed for you, and we bonded, yes, true
A deeper, stronger bond than with Elmer's glue

Sometimes looking at you is like seeing a show
You are beautiful, yes, from head to toe

We were joyful when we heard your chosen name
Someday, you will hear of your grandma's love and fame

You are very serious with things you do
Copying Mommie, learning clue by clue

You are very strong, and this concerns me
Maybe you'll climb up a tall tree

Our duets on the piano are not for sale
We always enjoy piano without fail

In the rocking chair, milk bottle ends thirst
It's so comfy, but I never nod off first

You are always excited to see me again
I tally my blessings and am blessed amongst men

You and I share 100 percent trust my dear
Our love will only grow, it's clear

You act like Mom, it's so unreal
I've even heard your little girl squeal

You are so much like Mom, it's like reliving the past
Her childhood came, and away it then dashed

You and Mom are always special pals all day
When you have your nap, Mom then makes hay

When your daddy holds you, and your eyes meet
Volumes are spoken as your hearts greet

I'm your grandpa, and you make me glad
My love is different from your loving dad

Your toys are fun as you remove them from nook
Some get pondered, and others forsook

You love books, and one has no libel
God's spirit spoke this one called the Bible

You put words together, but I can't know
All the thoughts and meanings under that pretty bow

You use a booster chair, yes, and yipes
Those high chairs are only for little tykes

You love to copy me in word and deed
You say amen at the end as creed

I'm fifty-eight years older, and that won't change
When you're ten, and I'm sixty-eight, will I look strange?

I have three women, and each stole my heart
You snagged mine right from the start

When together, you make my stresses melt away
Leaving isn't any fun 'cause I'd really rather stay

Words can't explain what being with you means
I'm so proud of you, I'm busting buttons and seams

Cute to see you as you kick a ball
Sometimes you didn't want it to go that way at all

When I'm with you, my work is out of mind
There is no thought of getting behind

I'll remember all the times you run to me so fast
Lord, you know I want childhood to last and last

I toast you, my princess, with these simple words
May you love the Savior, see stars, and listen to birds

⌒ ⌒ ⌒ ⌒ ⌒ ⌒ ⌒ ⌒ ⌒ ⌒ ⌒

Written on occasion of precious Taryl's second birthday party. 'Twas happy
to be part of this grand time. Now I'll have time to write something for
number three year. Love you, Taryl, and remember I carry you in thoughts
and heart.

⌒ ⌒ ⌒ ⌒ ⌒ ⌒ ⌒ ⌒ ⌒ ⌒ ⌒

Moma-sita-monalisa-aromita-liromea

Momma dearest, your title is so long
Sounds like part of an operatic song

You left this castle for a site
North country beauty is so right

This abandoned mode does not fit
Pray thee, my queen, why you split?

My flag of surrender, fly from tower
Domestically leaves me sour

Wearing my cleanest dirty shirt
Tonight, it will burden more dirt

I call your name and echoes down to dungeon
I eat a raw runniuon

Not tired to sleep in my chambers
Moon and stars help my inner lamebers

I must ride all night to you, my queen
Drawbridge won't work ov'r alligats creen

Holy book comforts ye candle burns down
Your return a celebration to crown

Your portrait fills my mind and heart dear
Soon I'll have you near.

~ ~ ~ ~ ~ ~ ~ ~ ~ ~ ~

Written on occasion of thinking about Bobbi up at Karen's and her joy shared with Karen, Jordan, Taryl, and J.T. They are an award-winning family, and I'll be up there soon too. The licorice kid.

~ ~ ~ ~ ~ ~ ~ ~ ~ ~ ~

Lauren, Our Rose

Thanks for coming to see me at my place
I understand you love my room and lace

I looked at you, and you said nice big eyes
I was little compared to adult size

Come back and see gains I have made
I sleep well inside or outside with shade

I saw you jump up and try to be first
Whenever my demeanor changed to burst

You told Grandma to look at my little toes
You loved me 'cause you beep-beeped my nose

If I were to choose a grandpa just for me
He would be just like you, you see

When we first met, I tried to make a good impression
It was a big moment for us—this first session

Your rocking and singing were great
Can't remember if I kept you up late

When we met, I wanted to do a twirl
Newborn first and then a bigger girl

My blanket is such a nice silk
Excuse me—I'm being served milk

My daddy is a lot like you, grandpa dear
Your voices sound so good in my ear

I have a cousin named Taryl, the sweet
Meeting her will be a delight and neat

I've recently learned to smile at Mom and Dad
Didn't know there was such power to be had

My brother holds my hand while in the car
I love him, and he loves me both near and far

This house surrounds me and the changes fit
Floors and door and refrigerator were a hit

My babyhood is so much work for my staff
A real happy time is when I take my bath

Don't know how I got here and have no fright
Glad I wasn't downloaded from a how-to site

My schedule is working and sleeping for three hours
Mommie is so blessed—should I order in flowers?

Demanding and, yes, can I be so very bold?
My favorite time is when you give me a hold

When I awake, I want to be debriefed on issues
Most issues make me cry, so pass the tissues

You report my gains, it's always great news
Is anyone aware that I'm planning a world cruise?

I'm so happy with my family, I could shout with glee
I already know they love me so unconditionally

You and Grandma sang a song you chose
In this song, I was mighty like a rose

    ~ ~ ~ ~ ~ ~ ~ ~ ~ ~ ~

Written on occasion of meeting my precious little Lauren for the first time. The togetherness was so good, and we had loads of fun. Our hearts swell with love and pride as we see you and think and pray for you. Grandpa Tom and his bride, Grandma.

    ~ ~ ~ ~ ~ ~ ~ ~ ~ ~ ~

Trucking On

The old wheel was getting tiresome
I have traveled a lot of miles

On this flat road, the tires do hum
Almost there and with good smiles

Written on occasion of remembering the end of a journey.

My Lady Lauren

Put away fears of flying and flew
To see this lady Lauren so brand-new

New to me but already six months
It's now noon, and we are at lunch

She seems so happy all the time
Especially keen on up and climb

With lady in my arms—both secure
Very rarely did I behold a tear

Lord, take this time and really bless it
It's deeply wonderful but a short visit

Innocently trusting and bright eyes
Growing fast but is just the right size

Grandpa fed you and pretty soon
I'd wipe your chin with the handy spoon

With eyes closed, I held you and prayed
Little angel, you receive the top grade

Mom and Dad—amazing—so lively and quick
They are experienced—have many a trick

Little princess, your desire for this hour?
Your smile brings camera—o what power!

Close eyes—rock in Daddy's strong arms
He kisses, hugs, and sings away harms

Grandpa must go now just as he came
In a big bird through sun or wind or rain

Whether I'm here or there, I love you true
Royal little princess—I miss you

~ ~ ~ ~ ~ ~ ~ ~ ~ ~ ~

Written on occasion of thinking about little baby Lauren. She brings me so much joy—big difference between a girl and a boy. God bless you, Lauren. And your grandpa will always love you at least 100 percent.

~ ~ ~ ~ ~ ~ ~ ~ ~ ~ ~

Put a Lid on It

The summer fruit dangles
Canning is not old fangles

Each jar of precious fruit
Opened later at snowy suit

Apricots, peaches, and plums
Children will eat and say yums

Lots of work goes into each jar
Day after day, do you feel par?

Put on the lid and then the ring
While jars are sealing, you sing

Opening the jar is a daily gift
Outside the snow is on a drift

Craving—don't go to a store
In the pantry are jars galore

Fresh fruit during winter's press
God's jars are more, not less

Putting lid on or taking it off
God's love we know is not aloft

Christmas colors abide in home
Special is the peach in its half dome

Bounty is rich, and bounty is true
Canned fruit keeps you from being blue

Put all the joy of summer in the jar
Open when Jack Frost sits on your car

Open a can from the wide shelf store
Home jars have mother's love and more

Fill a jar with peace, love, and needed charm
Pop the lid when trouble threatens harm

A message from Jesus comes at this juncture
Sins are sealed and can't open or puncture

Sin jars are in the pantry lost forever
Don't search for them, don't endeavor

Majestically, God parades the jars of fruit
Try your own plan, and you won't be cute

Open the wrong jar, and you eat deep remorse
Guilt, shame, and defeat make life coarse

Run to God's pantry, can that which has mar
Seal all those nasty thoughts in a mason jar

Soon that jar will be lost

∿   ∿   ∿   ∿   ∿   ∿   ∿   ∿   ∿   ∿   ∿

Written on occasion of remembering my Mom's hard work, the great tastes
in the winter, and how Christ removes our sins and they are lost forever.

∿   ∿   ∿   ∿   ∿   ∿   ∿   ∿   ∿   ∿   ∿

To Little Lauren Nordstrom

Shall I resumè or apply for the job at hand?
My experience as a grandpa is very good in this land

A little girl like you needs to know my stats
Please hire me for on call as a babysats

I know the routine for all the different stages
I even know any problems coming by gauges

I have thirty-two years experience with all levels of childhood
Your daddy is my best reference as to "he could"

A girl can't willy-nilly transfer her trust to a pop
Don't worry about that condition called "gray on top"

I bring to the job a desire to be thoroughly good
Strolling you in the breeze requires the hood

I do extra things but I would never accept your pay
When I rock you, and you fall asleep—I pray

My ability to love and cherish and protect is fact
When your mood swings south, I will certainly use tact

You are allowed to cry and throw in some sass
Is that smell for real, or do I mark it down as gas?

When I am with you alone and parents out for a twist
I actually follow to the letter everything on the list

When your little hand pulls on my beard or moustache
I'll be honored and endure the pain—with you no clash

I'll never leave you lonely—I'll stay close by your bed
Sometimes I'll say "Wow, Lord" and gently touch your head

Muffled phones and otherwise quiet will abide
When you are older, we'll play seek and hide

When your parents return and eagerly run in the door
My on-call grandpa job—is it supposed to be a chore?

It's an honor and privilege to spend time with you, Lauren
Knowing we might bond emotionally keeps me soar'n

My rocking chair pace is customized just for you
Names change in my stories, but they are really true

Good night, lil' wrangler asleep on the hay—I sing
Should I tell you that lil' girls grow up and ring?

You ask what is my weakness, and what can I do
I get sad and show it when saying bye to you

I'm available now should you decide me to employ
Lastly, I also have been known to bring a new toy

Written on occasion of the Thursday eve hours or days before Lauren's birth.
Do you hear all that cooing and baby talk? Well, that's the parents. I give
you to the Lord, little angel, and he will keep you just fine. God bless. The
on-call grandpa applicant, Poppa Tom.

Nains

Nains have wheels and click and clack
Old trains have smoke coming out their stack

Nains are exciting to me
Nains give me glee

Thomas's nains are fun for me
I'm between two and three

Daddy, Grandpa, and I love them so much
Some nains are small ones, and you can touch

From preschool, I dash to my room
My nain will be going pretty soon

Each nain car carries my wonder and dreams
I'm so proud of my nains, I could burst my seams

Only 2+ but I just figured out
Nains have a lot to learn about

Mom and Dad and I saw big trains in old town
I thrill all over when I hear their sound

The engine tells where to go and when
The caboose looks to see where we've been

Some car's haul oil and some haul freight
Many cars go from state to state

Car's haul people with babies that squeal
Then hungry people go to the car with a meal

Whoo a whoo ding ding, says the engine whistle
Passing through trees, flowers, creeks, and thistle

Nains sound very good on the flat or going steep
At night, many children listen and go to sleep

Nains have many homes, they are called a station
So many homes clear across the nation

Some cars to add, some cars to subtract
People in charge really need to know that

Don't know which one to watch or to ride
I'm happy to know them, it swells my pride

I listen to nains while on my grandpa's lap
It's better when I wear my engineer's cap

Real nains really look so Gigamos
My little nains are called Thomas

Nains are so wonderful, snakelike in motion
I learn a lot about nains with a notion

The nain now is leaving, and I hear all aboard
In my life, I want to be on the nain with my Lord

Some nains follow the dis track signs
My nain follows the tie that binds

Nains can even be found in parks
When the nain sounds, my dog barks

Nains are most fun, it is clear
Engineers really don't have to steer

Speak to me now, nain, whistle, please
Every time my daddy gives me a squeeze

Nains pull in to cheer or tear
I'll always want my nains to be near

When I look out the nain's window clear
New things to see always appear

New nains are shiny, someone wipes the dust
Old nains are weathered with plenty of rust

Don't know what I'll be, but I feel
A nain engineer looks like a very good deal

Time now to sleep, and I'm hitting the sack
Mommy and Daddy tuck me with love and no lack

The nain of life has its downs and steep
Hand on throttle and eye on rail, I'll keep

This nain will make it, I'm really, really sure
God and family love will help me endure

Nain bound for glory all in a row
People are missing, reaping what they sow

We're coming to the station, beautiful from here
Girls and boys running around with cheer

Now the station and the nain not a peep
I've drifted off to a wonderful sleep

Tomorrow, I'll awake, and after the room, I have scanned
You'll know, I love nains because I slept with one in my hand

     ∼   ∼   ∼   ∼   ∼   ∼   ∼   ∼   ∼   ∼   ∼

Written on occasion of remembering how much Logan loved trains that he
called Nains. Written for Logan and Jonathan from Grandpa Tom. I love
you guys with all my heart. Jonathan, this is just the beginning. More later.
Got to hurry. Here comes the sleep train . . . *zzzzzzzzzzzzzzzzz.*

     ∼   ∼   ∼   ∼   ∼   ∼   ∼   ∼   ∼   ∼   ∼

Son

A son is someone you have seen grow up
Sometimes you look at him using a cup

You are amazed at the things he can do
Often he seems just like you

You have watched him grow and mature
He now knows that love sickness has a cure

His family needs him, and so he goes to work
Some mornings he searches for a perk

Things wear out, and others go bad
He'll fix it, yes, that dear old Dad

He doesn't ride around on a steed and sword
He often needs wisdom, so he asks the Lord

At the dinner table, each sits in their place
Eating begins after Dad says the grace

Each talks with no interruption, please
Food passed around politely without tease

Now it's time for bed, but we're not finished playing
Dad speaks, we obey—lights out after praying

Judge and funmeister, he has them to combine
The sentence is meted after the tear and whine

He struggles hard, and all the bills get paid
His love for his family does grow never a fade

This son and dad now carry the yoke of headship
He's the one that tries to be fair with block and chip

Son now dad, lend me your ear
Decisions make through smile or tear

This house now home must have Jesus to lead
Unconditional love, forgiveness, and hope the creed

Son now dad, sometimes you dig and then dare
Remember, you are ideal because you are there

Hold your family close and love do measure
In your arms, abide the best/most valuable treasure

Written on occasion of Father's Day for Jonathan, Jordan, and Calvin. Thanks for being such awesome guys. I'll try not to get in your way, but remember, I'll not be too far away. Happy Father's Day!

Father, Daughter, Strong and Secure

Put the film on a backward roll
Far enough back to grip my soul

Play forward in slow motion, please
What a darling with hair in a tease

Rewind the part on the farm
Watch her smile and the cute charm

Pause—when I'm rocking her to sleep
Those scenes are cherished—I'll keep

So fast that she walked on her own
There she is—with an ice cream cone

Friends and activities really abound
I was her cheerleader going around

There we are during that big test
Giving you away in my tux and vest

Treasured memories—more on the way
Rerun that—our granddaughter at play

Jackson Thomas has my middle name
He's my pal in laughing or in game

Daughter and two children—nice show
Son-in-law makes it four in the snow

The past seems fast with a little blur
Father, daughter love so strong and secure

Written on occasion of thinking about how thankful to the Lord I am for such an awesome, beautiful, talented daughter, Karen. Close is only a thought away. Thoughts are sealed to the Lord with prayers. May all your problems be little ones.

Shuzz

Shuzz are fun
Especially in the sun

Some are tight
Some are just right

Shuzz make you happy
When ground is snappy

Velcro works fine
Laces are divine

Some shuzz have a face
Others help keep pace

Shuzz can be pretty
Make you feel giddy

When shuzz have a tongue
No air from the lung

Shuzz have a heel
Now let us kneel

All shuzz have a sole
Some soles have a hole

Certain shuzz are hard to fill
From heel to toe, I can try still

People are hard to understand
Why their shuzz fill with sand

Shuzz can make you go fast
Special shuzz last and last

Shuzz take you all around
Shuzz can make you bound

Interesting shuzz have lots of glitter
Tasting shuzz can be rather bitter

School shuzz and home shuzz and swim shuzz too
All have a purpose just for you

Decide which shuzz to use
Think about your don'ts and dos

Shuzz can keep you warm
I love their country charm

A lot of things you can lose
Keep track of those things called shuzz

Sleeping cozily now in my bed
No thought of my shuzz in my head

I'll never complain about this pair or that
I have feet that can walk or just tap

Someone without feet goes a slower pace
They could even have a smile on their face

Desiring shuzz that are so fancy
Could reveal something that's chancy

God loves you from the top of your squeal
Right down to the sole and heel

Good night now and do not fear
Your shuzz won't leave, they'll be right here

My shuzz are ready, and no pay request
Care to shuzz will look the best

Bye for now, climb another rung
Be careful not to step on the tongue

Running sometimes causes sad faces
When we forget to tie our laces

Shuzz don't need things like locks
Just need companion socks

Which pair will you wear for that affair?
Some might show that you dare

Shuzz of old go to throwaway
Memories of goings just don't sway

Shuzz are just shuzz that is the rule
Something old sometimes and something jewel

Step into the carriage of horse not gas
So glad your shuzz are not of glass

Shuzz can also go pedal to the metal
Too fast can cause one to sweat-el

Feet can say, "Wait—those shuzz don't fit"
To the store, another pair to get

Be my friend and come in for a while
Can you walk in my shuzz for a mile?

So ends this saying without clues
I go along loving my shuzz

Written on occasion of my angel Taryl referring to shoes as Shuzz.

Mom—Hold Me Close for the Picture

Mom, or should I say mother dear
In your womb—your love was clear

Now that I'm born, and your milk sustains
Every day I try so hard to make gains

Can't thank you enough for swaddle
Will I be spoiled with all your coddle?

My heart fills with peace in your arms
Your humming is just one of your charms

Noticed when you carried me to my room
I had lots of clothes and toys going zoom

During my surgery soon, I'll do what I can
Not a big deal—I'll face it like a man

Thanks for the nine-month ride in your womb
I got big and simply needed more room

Mom—hold me close for the picture
Guess you know I am a permanent fixture

Don't understand how you can love me so much
You give so much—know you love me—by touch

Love to drink from you—they call it nurse
Can't compare to that container—in your purse

Will your love always be—or will you run out?
Thanks, thanks—your love with me has high clout

Mom—hold me close for the picture, please
I'm a tough guy—you can give me a gentle squeeze

I love you, Mom, from your head to your toes
Your loving fingers caress my eyes and nose

Mom, I forever and ever give you my total heart
Your love makes me grow in every little part

Special and precious are my names for you, Mother
God chose you for me, and who would want another?

Your love is the best I've had in my whole life
I'm so happy I could play a drum or blow a fife

Mom—hold me close—shutter is about to snap
This picture is good—with me sitting on your lap

Here I am getting sleepy again—turn down lights
You treat me so well that I have no gripes

I'm okay, Mom—I am so alert in my lil' ole head
You are tired, Mom—why don't you go to bed?

You are wondering—what will my life be like
After the surgery—I'll be improved as a tyke

Is there something I can help you with? I wonder
Please help me with new words—what is a blunder?

Many pictures of you and I—keep your eyes dry
People come over and say, "My, what a guy"

Thanks, my precious mom—you'll never know
The depth of my love—now watch it grow and grow

⌐ ⌐ ⌐ ⌐ ⌐ ⌐ ⌐ ⌐ ⌐ ⌐ ⌐

Written on occasion of remembering the hugs and prayers for J.T. and his
parents. God saw us through this.

⌐ ⌐ ⌐ ⌐ ⌐ ⌐ ⌐ ⌐ ⌐ ⌐ ⌐

Nemo

My little fish came to live with me
He swims around and shows such glee

He knows his borders, and they are glass
Movements are sometimes like dash

He always looks busy and seems happy
Wonder if he wants to go and look for pappy

His house is all one window—no walls
No steps, no stairs, no railings—no falls

I'll give him a tour of my big house
He won't be interested in chasing a mouse

I can run and jump and climb all day
But I can't stay underwater—his way

His freedom is limited yet seems carefree
No thoughts of schooling and a degree

Is he lonely in there all by himself?
He moves around and is quite stealth

Tomorrow is the day he gets a new friend
Any loneliness now will be on a mend

Love my trains, books, and fish that looks
He doesn't bathe, comb, and never cooks

Little Nemo, I love you that's what I say
Here's your food—do you want to pray?

I'm older now with responsibilities and such
Mom and Dad say now I'm grown up so much

Feeding time will always be before I eat
Two times a week, you can expect a treat

I'm sleepy now and, after my napping, dose
We'll talk some more with my nose close

Your first day, my heart, you really won
I said to Mom and Dad I like it that one

My friends all want to see you for sure
None of them will use bait and a lure

Good night, Nemo, while moonbeams dance
Seeing you happy is my sleepy last glance

Mom and Dad kiss me goodnight and tuck chin
They hold hands and walk with a coy grin

⁓ ⁓ ⁓ ⁓ ⁓ ⁓ ⁓ ⁓ ⁓ ⁓ ⁓

Written on occasion of Logan getting a pet fish. He was so happy, and it was so awesome to hear him on the phone. I was thrilled to share in his excitement. God bless you, Logan, as you experience each moment of each day. Thanks for being my little buddy.

⁓ ⁓ ⁓ ⁓ ⁓ ⁓ ⁓ ⁓ ⁓ ⁓

The Winner's Circle

The hushed crowd awaited the MC
Tomorrow it will be available on PC

This much-anticipated time was at hand
Soon the winner would rise and stand

Against all odds with a lot of verve
This person of steady focus and nerve

The MC takes out an envelope and smiles
The winner is someone with hard miles

The name is announced, and the audience rises
This person is getting the top of the prizes

The deafening roar of the crowd swamps him
Yet he walks to the stage fit and trim

His little boy hugs his mommie as tears cascade
Her happiness and tears her husband has made

He steps to the mike and attempts a dim of the din
He says thank-you, and the crowd's noise will win

Finally, they allow him to speak without applause
I've worked hard, prayed, and followed the laws

The crowd begins to chant, "Korie, Korie, Korie, Korie"
She goes to the front with emotion from her quarry

Seeing them both embrace and express a kiss
Causes the crowd their senses to miss

She steps back and allows him to try to speak
Flashes going off and reporters on the sneak

The crowd hangs on every word that he says
All of it is truth and not a word of jes

Across the land, young people huddle to TV
Their hero Jon is someone they want to be

They begin to chant his name now and louder
When this is over, they'll sit and ponder chowder

An attendant brings Logan to the stage
The crowd goes crazy and akin to a rage

This is the son of this heroic, awesome Jon
The crowd chants, "Logan, Logan, Logan, Lo-gon

They blow kisses to their adoring fans
Security helps them exit out past the bands

Tight security and limos help in their escape
Behind them now are the cameras and tape

I feel like a hero on a horse and holding sword
I'm blessed to have family and my precious Lord

What was the award that caused this jubilee?
Passing the test for the national registry

Pulled into the driveway all was quiet hurray
Logan hugged Jon saying be like you someday

Thank you, son, and to the award I'm adoren
When precious Korie gives me my little Lauren

⌐ ⌐ ⌐ ⌐ ⌐ ⌐ ⌐ ⌐ ⌐ ⌐

Written on occasion of Jonathan passing the national registry test for
paramedic. The family is thoroughly proud of him and can now breathe

a little easier after this waiting time for the test results. His first response was "Thank you, Jesus!" God answers prayer. To God be the glory—great things he has done. In his time, he makes all things beautiful. Oh yes, and Proverbs 3:5, 6.

Is the Skylight?

I went up on my roof to repair
Those old skylights oh to stare

New ones touted were energy star
The old ones discolored and with mar

At night, I would like to see stars
Old ones discolored and with scars

New ones purchased and good deal
Now the stars will look so very real

Friend and ladder and quality time
Soon new skylights will look so fine

Removed the old ones ugly to the core
Installed the new ones—a steady chore

Holding on—safety rope—prepping to fit
The new skylights—made a swell hit

On top of my house—I thanked the Lord
There was my family looking up and skyward

Tools put away and the job is all done
New skylights are ready for dark or sun

Muscles are sore and tight from tension
Do you mind that I make that a mention?

Look, Daddy, I can see the top of the trees
Skylights show trees moving—in breeze

Is the sky light—can I hold it in my hand?
My children think everything is grand

Skylights in—saved money—didn't get hurt
Moved cautiously, steadily always alert

On the housetop so lively and so quick
Holding on while working—no simple trick

All that behind me, I'm checking the honeydew
My, oh my, I'm ready for a break—time did flew

While on the housetop I had no bag of gifts
Knowing my family is happy—my spirit lifts

Remember now my wife said don't be a clown
If you don't feel safe up there, come down

I'll be sore for a while—don't feel just right
Job wasn't heavy because it was just skylight

Written on occasion of thinking how proud I am of Jonathan our son. He is
able to fix anything and takes pride in his work. His lovely wife, Korie, and
awesome son, Logan, and Princess Lauren all enjoy all the work Jon does on
the house. Korie certainly does her share also. Now the only time you'll hear
honeydew is when no. 3 child is announced! Logan and Lauren, are you in
favor of that? Can you see them praying as youth begins repose? Just before
parents leave the room and after the kisses are placed, Logan can be heard
asking, "Daddy, is the skylight? How can one answer this little dear?

Fency Fence

There it was the bare ground
Traveled by squirrel and hound

Two little tots know no fear
A fence 'twas needed, it's clear

Would miss viewing woody fern
This would end nervous discern

Gate is locked, world is there
Won't look for hide nor hair

Run, run or blow, bubbles, blow
Run with a hat or a hair bow

Mom can relax—you are in yard
Hears your voices—yet on guard

Dad remembers all the work
No dangers in the yard—lurk

Each post each screw and nail
He finished the fence—no fail

He leaves for work—children safe
Only Mommie opens the gate

Children, learn boundaries in life
Inside fence is less, less strife

Today your lil' friend will be guest
Play in yard—go north, south, or west

Play yard is happy just now
Tots imagine a horse, dino, or cow

Fency, fancy, friendly formed fence
No monsters here not even for pence

Tots play and Mom and Dad hug
The feeling is . . . yes, it's snug

Dinner is ready, wash hands now
They come in with hesitant brow

'Twas worth all the work and pay
Tots are safe—and it's safe to say

Gaith and boards, my border tell
In my yard, I can laugh and yell

     ～ ～ ～ ～ ～ ～ ～ ～ ～ ～ ～

Written on occasion of remembering helping Jonathan begin the fence project. We had to leave for home in California, but we knew he would finish it. He filled his spare time with the fence, and it looks smart. He took a break and had coffee and tart. We loved working together and knew our safety goal for the children was a priority. Thanks son for the chance to work with you again. Never was a tantrum to toss because we both were the workers and both were the boss. Wonderful to work together and get things done. Just in time for the darkness to win over the sun. Yes, fency fence you are, and you are way above par. God bless you richly.

     ～ ～ ～ ～ ～ ～ ～ ～ ～ ～ ～

What Does the Baby Say?

The youngest of the brood is asleep
When awake to run and even to leap

What doth she say being the latest?
Does she love vegetables or hatest?

What pleases her when mood is rough
Is it true she wears feelings on cuff?

What's that sound as she tapers to nap?
Humming and singing—don't call it rap

Becoming very advanced can tie shoes
She plays with dolls—with ne're blues

Out of high chair and bib in the drawer
She is happy whether a reaper or sower

Don't worry she can hold her own ground
Not selfish but requests, and yup, a pound

Is she the baby? Well, she's my young sis
Did you upset her and now just to hiss?

Generous of heart and sincere of smile
Will listen to ye and will walk a mile

Driving her car having peace with God
Irritant others get a smile and a nod

She's home from work with feet in air
Relaxing and closing eyes now that's fair

It's her birthday today—chocolate good
Cake and candles and balloons and pud

Time to blow out candles—how many, lady?
Seriously only one 'cause you are the baby

Sit down a spell and open card
Has no batter, no flour, or lard

Words are homespun—ev'r part
Cooked up and warm from heart

Sit back and just count the ways
God has blessed these many days

Joyous singing and cake on fork
You came to us—not by a stork

God chose you for me and me—you
No need to wonder—love you true

You are my Klaris, and I am your Tom
Thanks, Lord, we are both a Nordstrom

      ～   ～   ～   ～   ～   ～   ～   ～   ～   ～   ～

Written on occasion of thinking about my lil' sis Klaris. We are very close, and I cherish that relationship. Very close to Connie and Bill also. I hope she has a super birthday, and that there will be some surprises along the way. Birthday of happiness and full of the joy of the Lord.

      ～   ～   ～   ～   ～   ～   ～   ～   ～   ～   ～

Creak and Creak Again

It is ready for duty, oh yes
The power to run is engineless

We call it rocking to and fro
A chair for nursing or to sew

This chair has been—many years
Witnessed laughter and tears

Grandpa rocks babies to sleep
Eyes closed soon not a peep

Snow falls on the outside world
Baby feels rocking while curled

Babies trust as chair creaks again
Grandpa strokes his beard on chin

Blanket wrapped and feeling snug
This session is one long hug

Next comes prayers, kisses, and a tuck
Everything can wait—even rubber duck

Trains and books and dolly with open eyes
Creak and creak for Grandpa's rockabyes

⌐ ⌐ ⌐ ⌐ ⌐ ⌐ ⌐ ⌐ ⌐ ⌐ ⌐

Written on occasion of remembering our daughter Karen jumping in my lap at age thirty-one and exclaiming, "Dad, I remember that creaking of the old rocking chair." When the world is coldhearted and hope has lost its flair—remember the creaking comfort of the old rocking chair. Memories will be evoked as the chair begins its theme. Close your eyes and of childhood begin a dream. Of this, you might find a picture in your purse. Never forget it's here you learned to nurse. Thanks, Mother. Excuse me now. I hear a creaking sound that needs me.

Code in My Head

The ambulance sped off as if in battle
Some items on the inside began to rattle

Code was now in effect, and it was in my head
Preparation and practice went on ahead

My thoughts were that someone had life
But staying alive was priority strife

The crew looked to me to be the lead
Confidence was a companion to speed

Elderly man already status dead
All methods to help were instead

Items were quickly pulled from the kit
No time to lazily just sit and sit

Events flew by like a movie going forward fast
Thankful now for this experience that will last

Times like this when eternity doors open wide
Adrenalin valves are open fully on my inside

Doing all a paramedic can do and yet
This person heaven or hell will get

We were there to offer the last hope
This man was certainly at end of rope

Lord, thank you for helping me lead the crew
Your presence with me I really knew

Lord, I need your wisdom and guidance for sure
Through all of this, I will certainly endure

Hot food now inside and a warm bed to repose
So tired now and paperwork done, here I doze

Yes, Lord, yes, Lord, you and I did our bit
This is the real thing, no longer a skit

Tomorrow, if asked to lead, I'll not stall
I am living your touch on my life—my call

⁓ ⁓ ⁓ ⁓ ⁓ ⁓ ⁓ ⁓ ⁓ ⁓ ⁓

Written on occasion of thinking about the stress and emergency situations
to which our awesome Jonathan responds.

⁓ ⁓ ⁓ ⁓ ⁓ ⁓ ⁓ ⁓ ⁓ ⁓ ⁓

Grandpa, Do You Love Me?

Amazed and awestruck over you
Three grandchildren—and now you

Special and precious you be you
Cute and interesting things you do

Gift from God, and I love you so
I love you from your head to a toe

Will always love you—Grandpa's word
Let that be so clear—and never blurred

Breathing is good and steady heart
Grandpa loved you from the start

Homemade songs have same theme
Tell of you being my lil' sunbeam

Love is what I want you to know
Love implanted in heart as you grow

You are asleep, and I close my eyes
Special and precious is your size

Look in my eyes, and I see bundled joy
Yes, grandpa loves you—little boy

Getting stronger every day—thanks, Lord
Soon you'll be running—see a Ford

God has given you the best family
Situation proceeds so very handily

I pray for you and never stop
This harvest of love—what a crop

Grandpa loves you—it's a new song
I'll be there soon—won't take long

Mountains in life—sure as a dime
Only option for us—start to climb

My tape measure is ready—yes, oh
As I'm holding you—I see you grow

Warm and soft—and such tiny shoes
When you visit, it's big, big news

Train up a child in the right way
With Jesus as Savior—less stray

Given to the Lord—worry much less
Moment by moment, we give our stress

It's time to nurse—I hand you to Mom
God's plan for nutrition was aplomb

In the driveway—I wave good-bye
Joyful spirit and no tear in eye

Phone calls later, more joy flows
Missing him, and no one really knows

Yes, Grandpa loves you and ensured
Wonderful time is sharing God's Word

Toss the airplane, let it soar high
Don't worry about others—just try

Grandpa wants to walk—climb a tree
The air is fresh and fun—away from TV

Something old—something weird or odd
Maybe walk barefoot over cold sod

Let's sit by the water for a long spell
Ask a question—my best answer, I'll tell

Time spent together is just so great
I'll race you home—it's getting late

You close your eyes at table for grace
Sleeping soon in bed with an angelic face

You stood in my shoes for a picture today
I trust you'll see God through me, I pray

Sun has descended and darkness a guest
Little man, you make Grandpa want a rest

You are excited about everything at once
One thing at a time is best—that's my hunch

I'm happy when you are here—I do say
Com' on, pal, let's go to town in the model A

Written on occasion of thinking about little Jackson Thomas Russell. So many
emotions and highs and lows, but he is doing well, and I am looking forward
to having a lot of fun with him as he grows up. I love each of my grandchildren
the very same and pray for each of them. When the day is done, I want them
to see God through my life. Nothing else matters that much because having a
close relationship with Jesus matters most when everything else will pass away.
God bless, Logan, Taryl, Lauren, and Jackson—in order of appearance—four
little people and only one lap. Yes, they'll fit and what a big moment. Smile
for the camera. Hold still. Now it's Grandma's turn. Korie or Karen, turn
the oven down, the pie might burn. Call the guys in from under the hood.
That Henry Ford made a product that was good. All around the table, the
blessing is said and then . . . Grandpa counts noses and, yes, there are ten.

Handy Foot

Four months and learning a new
Discovered my foot—something to chew?

I can stand on my mommy's lap
A foot can be used to *tap tap tap*

Today I held my foot in my hand
I'm the most clever in this land

Can't count my toes, but they are there
Sometimes I hold my foot up in the air

I make little gains and not too fast
I want Mommy's attention to last and last

Let's try this again—hand grabs foot
Is hand a branch and my foot a root?

I'll need my feet for lots of things
Siblings jump—do they have springs?

This hand and foot have me all worn out
Now Mr. Sandman, and I will have a bout

During intermission, I'll gain more strength
Watch very closely—I'll gain in length

This hand and foot thing—heavenly, you know
Mommy is taking pictures and is all aglow

⌐ ⌐ ⌐ ⌐ ⌐ ⌐ ⌐ ⌐ ⌐ ⌐ ⌐

Written on occasion of my little darling Kaitlyn's new skill and how much
I love her. We leave this scene as Daddy Jonathan comes in from work to
hear all the news. They sit around the dinner table and after the prayer begin

to take turns speaking. Logan tells of finding a little frog on his bike, and Lauren tells of reading a book, and Mom tells of Kaitlyn grabbing her foot. Jonathan gives Korie a lingering hug and thanks her for giving her these three gems. Soon another new day and adventures to cherish. And Grandpa Dumptruck wishes he could join them.

A Request for More Time

The birthdays come and go
They look and act like snow

Beautiful and party like right now
Soon to melt and then they bow

Next on stage is one of experience
Things handled now with endurance

Last year on things, I thought smart
Now again learning will start

Put me, Lord, as if in a fort
Keep me joyful and not out of sort

This year will be different, agree?
People around me will really see

No more commanding with a bark
Most times joyful as a lark

Fifty-nine is a nice number not even tho
Any number can carry a glow

Last piece of cake gets smaller
Candles now are not taller

Who is that person in the mirror?
The glass is clean not even a smear

That person is familiarly the same
In my heart, I am now more tame

Blessed by the Lord and so grateful
I have two children and one mate—tell

⌐ ⌐ ⌐ ⌐ ⌐ ⌐ ⌐ ⌐ ⌐ ⌐ ⌐

Written on occasion of reflecting on how brief life is and birthdays come
and go.

⌐ ⌐ ⌐ ⌐ ⌐ ⌐ ⌐ ⌐ ⌐ ⌐ ⌐

Step Up

Grandpa, walk with me—okay?
Walk with me, what do you say?

Proud to, oh little man
Okay then, hold my hand

Carefully now as we climb hill
Don't want to take a spill

Grandpa, I watch you step up
Next to you, I'm a little pup

Thank you for helping up this hill
Love you, Grandpa, you are a thrill

I watch you step—I hear your voice
Following you is my real choice

You say life is a continual stepping up
Obedience brings an overflowing cup

Follow God as you keep stepping up
Don't bark at God, oh precious pup

Yes, I will help you, my little man
I will pray for you—understand

Jesus stepped up and gave salvation
The foot of the cross—sweet location

I cherish you, my precious little pal
My feet seem big but only for a while

I want to have you proud of my steps
My mistakes will be learning debts

Admire my steps—and my buttons burst
I always want to put my Jesus—first

~   ~   ~   ~   ~   ~   ~   ~   ~   ~   ~

Written on occasion of walking with grandson J.T. and noticing he was looking back and forth from his little feet and my big ole gunboats. It was a Kodak moment, and one I'll never forget. I want to always be a loving grandpa to J.T. and my other four grandchildren. I'll need help though and so that's why God made prayer and also made a helper for Grandpa—called Grandma dearest.

~   ~   ~   ~   ~   ~   ~   ~   ~   ~   ~

Shine on, Son

Our son doth shine often
His smile hearts do soften

His wife is charming and witty
Has two children, dog, and kitty

Stars shine, and he is one
Proud to call him our son

His birthday came on schedule today
Wanted to see him but too far away

He shines at home and shines at work
His family is safe while shadows lurk

His sacrifices are rewarded each day
They all four practice and pray

Childhood memories really do shine
This hero/son is towing the line

Special and precious labels that fit
This man now a home run doth hit

He's worked hard and goals have won
Question is, when you coming home, son?

~ ~ ~ ~ ~ ~ ~ ~ ~ ~ ~

Written on occasion of Jonathan Douglas Nordstrom's thirty-third birthday. Words can't convey how I feel about him, but he knows I believe in him, and I know he believes and lives in the Savior, Jesus Christ. Though three thousand miles apart, we are bonded in love and are really close by. God bless you, son, and know your mom and I pray for you every day.

~ ~ ~ ~ ~ ~ ~ ~ ~ ~ ~

Princess Lauren Nordstrom

I'm about four inches long
My mom and dad sing a song

The song is from the heart
From down in the serious part

This song is sung without words
This song causes blood to surge

In four months, I'll arrive small
Soon after to want to crawl

My heartbeat has been heard
People listen and ner a word

I'll arrive with a lot of clout
Cuteness pervades with no doubt

My wonderful dad is called Jon
Is that right? Sometimes called Hon

Korie, my mom, has given a nine-month ride
With my parents, I want to abide

Who is that boy that just hit his noggin?
Wow, he's my very own brother Logan

Things will be great but get this straight
I'll want to eat and don't be late

My diapers shall be absorbent and soft
All dangerous things away and aloft

My milk I like not too hot or too cold
Am I sounding demanding or too bold?

I want to be held several times a day
Especially good when the chair does sway

When I go to bed I want it quiet! Period
Things to dream about—oh, such a myriad

Clean clothes are a must—or I'll fuss
Touch my face but my hair, I want no muss

Sing to me, please, about the Christian life
I want to know how to handle strife

Logan, I need you to put up with my mopes
I love you, my brother, you give me hopes

Who's that older guy sitting over there?
Can he be your sub in the rocking chair

Who is that woman with the sparkly smile?
Can we play piano for a while?

Princess, dear, over here—sit others dear
They also love you, it is so very clear

Jordan is your uncle—Karen is your aunt
Jordan is a fireman, and Karen bakes bant

Who is that little girl doing that cute twirl?
That's Taryl, your cousin—cookie batter a swirl

Going out in the car—entourage of at least two
Careful with my royalness, other drivers too

Mom, I'll be your pal—teach me this and that
Soon we'll shop for a hat and mat

Dad your faithfulness to us teaches me lots
Mr. Right like you, or my affection for him stops

Starting now with my royalness routine
If I get dirty, then you get to make me clean

Pictures won't be taken before midday nap
Please don't scare me with a flash, pop, or snap

Baby me, please—I'm soft as a kitten
Winter weather, I require on each hand a mitten

I'll be happier in a bath of water deliciously warm
Happily, I'll play in an environment with no alarm

I'll present myself as a lady with lace
Thank God for that amazing grace

A little girl is a new idea in this awesome home
Logan, show me how to play with cloth and chrome

Excuse me, please, this girl wants to sleep
I'm so exhausted that the monitor will not peep

~ ~ ~ ~ ~ ~ ~ ~ ~ ~ ~

Written on occasion of welcoming little Princess Nordstrom into my heart.
I already love you and assure you that with your parents' permission, I'll
tenderly rock you and sing some songs. Night, night little angel!

~ ~ ~ ~ ~ ~ ~ ~ ~ ~ ~

Wrapping It Up

Training still on and going full bore
Nearing completion, what's in store?

Every day is closer to my goal
When home, I'll take a stroll

Dad and I and Logan will talk
Training here will not be a lock

Wrapping up here will happen soon
Finishing will be such a boon

I'll take it all with me for sure
Quest to be best was my lure

Vapor rub under my sore nose
As the odors rose and rose

I'll wrap up the sway to and fro
Top concern was to just go and go

I'll wrap up the crying of kin nearby
Patient on gurney now fly and try

There'll be room for the stress
No more, Lord, and no less

Tired and hungry will also fit
Memories packed to the limit

My travel pattern to the west
Loved ones hold to my chest

Soon I'll zip it all up
Then a new place to sup

Trust will go in my carry-on
God is pilot so I can yawn

Necessaries sent on ahead
My head fits my own bed

Wrap up all that I've learned
I love you, Lord, not spurned

Blessings counted, there'll be more
It's wrapped up and out the door

No looking back, it's better forward
Help me with the next step, Lord

Written on occasion of thinking about Jonathan's transition as he packs up soon, leaves school, and is ready to come home.

Boxing

The serious and careful carrying of that box
From a room and closer to the exit door

My movement is as stealth as a red fox
This is the last box and then we will soar

Everything is moved now and packed in the trucks
Final thing now is to shut and lock the door

Look out past, the future now, trots
We are either reapers or we are sowers

Our heart to the new door soon walks
Our little princess has mirrors and drawers

New place will have room for hens and cocks
They might be frightened by the sound of the mower

Some parts will house weeds and rocks
Climbing the hills, I'll use God's power

Morning after my security will be mocked
The cloth sounded as it gave a tore

I realize now this is like my ship has docked
All things now in their place I will store

The door opened, and opportunity knocked
I sit with my prince and princess on the floor

If I don't slow down, I'll lose my socks
Now I'm relaxed and my eyelids lowered

My mind says hurry up, but my body balks
My love for you, Lord, will never ever sour

⌐ ⌐ ⌐ ⌐ ⌐ ⌐ ⌐ ⌐ ⌐ ⌐ ⌐

Written on occasion of Jordan and Karen, and Jonathan and Korie moving all their belongings.

⌐ ⌐ ⌐ ⌐ ⌐ ⌐ ⌐ ⌐ ⌐ ⌐ ⌐

Our Granny Love

In 1912, ninth is where I love to live
Door opens for you from world's sieve

Most people wouldn't fit in here
They are too big from selfishness or sneer

This home is a mission and can't be denied
Many times when I pray I've even cried

Leave your self outside the door, please
Let it fall from your mind like some leaves

Join me, please, by my fireplace so calm
Can I share of God's love because it's a balm

Sit in my chair—the one that is one hundred years old
Don't worry it'll hold you well—be bold

Memories abound everywhere you can look
See that Bible verse in frame—it adorns my nook

People have come in after sizing through door
They often want to return for God's love and more

See all my grandchildren—I'm teaching them love
None stick in my door—I think of them as dove

My gift to the world is a sincere peace to share
My Jesus is certainly able, and I bask in his care

Today is a special gift because I see you approach
You are on foot—no need for a fancy coach

When I open God's Word, truths fly out
It's like each one is a butterfly on heart route

God's truth lands in your heart, sure and soft
Can you gently feel his power or are you too aloft?

The purity of my fire(place) shows you a fire clean
Open God's Word and receive what you are to glean

You have a choice—front room or kitchen table
No biases here—just friendship and love—no label

Look over here—a great artwork of grandchild of three
I love you grandma—here are butterflies—count and see

Each grandchild is special and has so many charms
Isn't officially dedicated until held in Granny's arms

Each cold morning, I sit by my little woodstove hot
God speaks to me here—right here in this spot

My home is a mission to those in need of prayer
Everyone is important—haven't yet seen mayor

After you fit through my door—sit down and rest
You are special and precious—Jesus wants best

I'm eager to tell you of my Savior—so true
I trust in him—not myself—that is my daily rule

I can't change you, but this is my humble retreat
You fit through door perfectly—elevate feet

Let's pray before you go—let's lift his name in praise
Jesus gives peace, power, and purpose in life's maze

Before you go—stand at window and see sunset show
God-sized gifts we can't describe but inside just glow

Your visit was special—there's a new song in my heart
Let's shop again for verses and comfort—from his mart

Bye for now—cookies for the road—joy you do bring
Sometime soon—fill me in—after making my phone ring

Careful out there in this world with its terrible chill
Trust Jesus and obey him and ask, "What is your will?"

Written on occasion of being at Granny (or Thollander's home). She is a servant of the Lord and radiates his love. It was special to be there overnight in her guest wing called "pilgrims rest." We really needed her gentle retreat and all its comfort because little Jackson Thomas Russell was to be born the next day, and no one knew his condition except one—the heavenly Father. We were loaded to the top with concern and all the wonderings. Thanks, Granny, for your peaceful ways. When we left, I stood in line and waited to hug you because God got there first.

It was a January cold, clear day
When Jackson Thomas came our way

I looked into his precious little face
And learned more of God's amazing grace

Two for the Table

Sun shone through as we sat
Pondering of this and that

Thirty-six years of marriage
Our horse has a good carriage

Sparkling day out with hues
Blessings too many to choose

We count some blessings from God
The last rain nourished the sod

Eye contact and hands in soft grip
We shared I love you and then a sip

Drink and dessert in happy place
Won't forget this memory to trace

Purpose-driven life is such search
Much more than a bird on a perch

This time together at this address
Alone together and away from stress

Memories abound from yesterdays
Look at me for a little longer gaze

You are the angel I loved and chose
You are the beauty in garden of rose

Moment of peace in this table setting
When I am away, I will be regretting

You by my side I feel very complete
Happy are we in cold or high heat

Sharing experiences and laughing too
Forever together with love as glue

No matter what—I need your touch
You see, my dear, I love you very much

Away from you, I feel somewhat sad
Returning though will make me glad

Talking together with a happy tone
Less miles apart when on the phone

God guided me to you out of the rest
He knew I needed someone and the best

You are keeping my heart—away or home
Fix my collar and run hair with comb

You'll fill just one plate for a while
I'll come back going mile after mile

Plane leaves runway—eagle in flight
Praying for safety with all my might

Returning I'll be about the same size
We'll hug and kiss—you are my prize

Jesus, my Savior, mansion waiting too
Sins forgiven—want to glorify You

Plane lands on another part of earth
New joys and events give birth

Family is priority and very close
They give a good emotional dose

Love is a remedy for many an ill
It's just in time and never lies still

God's care while I'm gone, dear
We'll both be fine it is so clear

Home again and before I unpack
Hug me, and on cheek give a smack

Let's go to the table in corner for two
We'll hold hands and smile through

Comfort me, darling, at two for table
You are special and precious—your label

As we are bound to each other
There will never be another lover

All I want is to know of God's grace
Rest of my life to look into your face

       ◡   ◡   ◡   ◡   ◡   ◡   ◡   ◡   ◡   ◡   ◡

Written on occasion of leaving for five days to fly back to Virginia for our grandson's third birthday. The Lord provided the time off from work, but Bobbi won't be going with me. Two hearts beat as one, and while I am gone, I'll hear her heartbeat with mine. The cup runneth over with blessings. Just so you know, this is a surprise to Jonathan and Logan and four-month-old Lauren. Korie and I have a happy surprise for Jon when he arrives home from work. He told me his home was my second home and then asked when I was coming home.

       ◡   ◡   ◡   ◡   ◡   ◡   ◡   ◡   ◡   ◡   ◡

Leaves of Leisure

Logan—young man you love triking
When you pedal, you say biking

I was there on morn, cool and bright
Pedaling to you seemed so very right

We drove through leaves on Leisure Court.
No leaf the same—many colors in sort

Couldn't believe you pedaled so fast
Legs too short—on time before last

You love adventure—this we can talk
Once in a while, you would pick up a rock

You learned to stop when Grandpa said
Safety rules first—no pain on the head

Grandpa piled leaves—a pedal challenge
You pedaled through—no loss of ballenge

Your birthday came on that Sunday soon
You loved your nice remodeled bedroom

I see you going to church with tie and vest
Then I see your new bed, helping with rest

Your "Hi, Poppa" on phone makes my day
Soon Lauren will have words to say

You have the best parents on this earth
God chose them for you—and then a birth

Here is gem—requires no gold coin in purse
Each day rely on God—find a great verse

Logan, you have two jobs—son and brother
Learn love from your father and mother

Leaves on leisure and impromptu fun
Awesome memories in my mind do run

At high noon, you look west—I'll look east
I'm three hours behind, and your time increased

We'll get together and what a real blast
Bring your imaginary ship with tall mast

Logan, your value to me goes beyond measure
A grandson like you is such a serious treasure

⌁ ⌁ ⌁ ⌁ ⌁ ⌁ ⌁ ⌁ ⌁ ⌁ ⌁

Written on occasion of thinking back on my visit in Virginia during Logan's birth-week celebration. We are such pals, and I miss him totally beyond 100 percent. All the good times I can say so clear—fit now in happy memories and watered with a tear.

⌁ ⌁ ⌁ ⌁ ⌁ ⌁ ⌁ ⌁ ⌁ ⌁ ⌁

Jumping Jamboree

A woman am I with two energetic kids
I provided a home and put on lids

Things changed several years ago now
My husband decided out to bow

I had no help at all from him
At times, things have been slim

My joy now is when the kids succeed
I've been there for every need

At times, I really need a break
Just give me sleep and then awake

I've worked so hard, I've done my part
Lord, give me a grateful heart

In January, a trip south there'll be
A long lost uncle for to see

Vallejo is where his house sits
We'll be happy to share tidbits

When all are in bed and asleep
Safe and secure this house will keep

Up and scurrying and ready to go
No moss could ever underfoot grow

The kids have demeanor or glee
Today is the jumping jamboree

~ ~ ~ ~ ~ ~ ~ ~ ~ ~ ~ ~

Written on occasion of Dania and her children staying with us overnight for a rabbit show.

~ ~ ~ ~ ~ ~ ~ ~ ~ ~ ~ ~

Touchdown

The plane came to a gentle stop
I'm home, I'm home, I'm home

Nervousness from my list did lop
Never from their arms, I want to roam

So tired on my bed, I could drop
Everything's happy, ner a groan

Martinellis bottle, we pop
Joys and smiles are sewn

    ⌒   ⌒   ⌒   ⌒   ⌒   ⌒   ⌒   ⌒   ⌒   ⌒   ⌒

Written on occasion of a long flight to see loved ones. Welcome home, son.
We love you. Mom and Dad's prayers are answered.

    ⌒   ⌒   ⌒   ⌒   ⌒   ⌒   ⌒   ⌒   ⌒   ⌒   ⌒

Forever

A word like this carries weight
One cannot put on it a date

Change has arrived and took time
It was worth the good and grime

Dull pencils, empty pens, and paper now yellow
Courage inside of me is a grand ole fellow

Graduation a stepping-stone, and I feel diced
One thing forever, the cornerstone is Christ

The word *forever* means more than you see
Sometimes you must pay the emotional fee

Take the fo and add letters for a word now
This new word *forward* causes us to bow

Rever is next and see reverse in your mind
Going back sees the mountain you climbed

Forward and reverse have a different motion
Each carries deep thoughts with helpful notion

Forward and reverse seem intelligently tame
Transition causes one to think they are same

Looking back shows me all that I've learned
God's faithful track record I have not spurned

Supply and demand did not arrive together
Their relationship, I knew, God would not sever

Needs were met on the climb just in time
I am one of the branches, and he is the vine

Reverse makes me humble in light of his grace
I go forward now with a joyful smile on my face

Forward is when we run on dreams and wonder
We seek the missing puzzle piece as we ponder

Degree in hand, Lord, what is planned
Comforting to know I'm in the hollow of your hand

Keep me calm, Lord, I still step in faith and love
I turn from chaos and fear and just see you dove

The ceremony arrives, and I have a notion
Am I in reverse or forward motion?

Relief abounds you can be sure
Only with you, Lord, did I actually endure

Reverse is good to help gather mental bearings
Forward makes me shout with lungs and larynx

Forward and reverse with letters lopped
Become forever, a word that can't be stopped

Thank you, Lord, these two motions are for me
I'll never stop learning with this master's degree

~ ~ ~ ~ ~ ~ ~ ~ ~ ~ ~ ~

Written on occasion of wishing I could be there for my loving sister Connie's
big ceremony, but as you said, we both will be there in spirit and heart. We
are forever looking forward.

~ ~ ~ ~ ~ ~ ~ ~ ~ ~ ~ ~

Schrudury

I know that all will be well
My knee makes me yell

Soon relief will be mine
You want me on time

Wouldn't miss it at all
Not me to halt or stall

Schrudury team just the best
Afterward I can really rest

During that time, I'll not grumble
They are taking away my stumble

Good as new from this trance
No, I'm not ready to prance

To the hospital, but not in truck
Driven by my loving Chuck

While I'm in there today
I'll from your heart never stray

When I'm back in this world again
All healed up and then I'll grin

Thank you for your support so clear
In my heart, you are so dear

     ~   ~   ~   ~   ~   ~   ~   ~   ~   ~   ~   ~

Written on occasion of my wonderful sister Klaris the evening before her surgery (schrudury) on her knee.

     ~   ~   ~   ~   ~   ~   ~   ~   ~   ~   ~   ~

Knee-d

Somewhere on a shelf on wall
To get there, I'll probably crawl

Frustration mounts as I read
Laid up and I am kneed

Husband scampers to and fro
Helps to bathroom, yes, I go

Modern tech made short order
This leg will not be shorter

I think about the mobility of ago
Now my demeanor takes some glow

On my back and getting bored
Praises are to him toward

Please get me this and then that
No need to get me my fancy hat

Now on crutches entering room
Not much time to comb and groom

Pills, chills, and dietary drills
Happy reminder insurance pays bills

Time from work, that's not bad
Deli can split and splat, I'm glad

Repaired, mended, and ready for trail
Came in second place to the snail

Each day passing, I take note
Leaping and running has my vote

Oh my's and sighs each sitting
Even these crutches my hands fitting

Not really hungry, not really tired
For now in this recovery, I'm mired

Phone calls and e-mails a little hurray
Tell me now, is it yesterday or today?

On this, I think my heavenly hope
Helps my purpose and my scope

No hurry and take my time
No grocery list, no nickel, no dime

Just now looking out window of clear
A really nice, happy day begins to appear

I'll be back in saddle high on hog
Now I'm thinking what a bump on log

I'll bounce back, it is no riddle
No sad songs from your fiddle

All green light carry on yes, indeed
Soon recovery over than normal speed

The body is so amazing—don't understand
Cellular teamwork together, they band

Instead of thinking, oh, what a grind
Be still and know He's there and kind

Doctor's orders sometimes seem mean
Especially when I use this ice machine

I know I'm grounded and seem just lazy
Soon I'll walk freely and pick a daisy

Excuse me, for now, I'm going to rest
Tell me, is anticipation or memory the best?

⁓ ⁓ ⁓ ⁓ ⁓ ⁓ ⁓ ⁓ ⁓ ⁓ ⁓

Written on occasion of my precious sister Klaris recovering from knee scoloperationalistic contrapulaitonables.

⁓ ⁓ ⁓ ⁓ ⁓ ⁓ ⁓ ⁓ ⁓ ⁓ ⁓

Welcome to My Place (with Addendum)

My home is not fancy
My food is not chancy

Wipe your feet of any grime
Mud on my floor is a crime

You are my guest
You will get my best

Don't compare me to wealth
Love here is open not stealth

Clean and bright with pillows fluffed
Not perfect—some things are scuffed

This is God's gift appreciated deeply
Tears of joy not long weeply

Every room is filled with memories of fun
Pictures on walls some fading from sun

Creaking floors, no longer grate me
Everything I thank God for gratefully

My greatest treasure is always in its place
The family Bible adorns the table with grace

The family album chronicles our living gifts
Looking at each picture, my soul lifts

All I could do for some things was mask it
Blessings are pressed down and overflowing from this basket

The roof doesn't leak, the drains work well
Sit for a while and some history I'll tell

Rocking chair creaks and has chipped paint
Grandchildren fell asleep there in their daint

Coffee, bacon, eggs by homemade bread
A symphony of smell slowly enters your head

Beds are soft and quiet but can't sleep late
Roosters crowing their schedule on slate

Firewood is a mixture of fir and oak
This stove works well with a stoke

As a kid in the Depression, I saved
Many things I wanted were shaved

Some things are saved for just in case
Cloth and cozies trimmed in lace

Learned to sew when times were really hard
Couldn't send but looked over new card

Cleaned houses as a girl for rich folk
Ate from their scraps of potato and yolk

Didn't have much for now, you see
Everything now I praise thankfully

Sewing things allow me to give
Giving helps me truly and joyously live

Come down in the basement and see
Fruit of my labor and liberty

I can lots of food for the winter months
Apricots especially add to a lunch

When my children from a visit leave
I give them fruit of my labor to cleave

Colorful jars of ring and lid are mason
All of that food was cleaned in my basin

Saturdays, we would just hop in our rig
Going to town was a welcome gig

Nest is empty and Daddy is gone
This life now is more pro than con

My status now is widow for sure
My Bible, my pictures, my memories do cure

Days of yesteryear I'd like to bring back
I sit still and never lose track

Happiness, happiness floods my mind
No thought of the daily grind

Our eldest son was killed in a car
Such a shock and a permanent scar

Just love me and take me as I am
Your joyous visit my thoughts will stem

I'm tempted to feel lonely, but why?
Life is to be lived after the cry

I go to bed now and feel a strong arm
It's Jesus with me for no harm

Tomorrow morning, the warm sunlight will shine through
My heart is full of precious treasures and I've things to do

Whatever tomorrow's tasks that are in my cart
Biggest chore of all is just making a start

Lord, help me always to reach out to the right
To the end, I will live for others with all my might

This rhyme is not finished because over time I'll add more
This helps express my love for Mom that I'll always adore

I love Dad too, and his rhyme is in the works
Thoughts of Mom and Dad, the tears from my heart and eyes jerk

It'll take a lifetime of adding to these lines
As the tool of recollection, my memories mines

What a priceless treasure of love and sacrifice they gave
Because of them my road of life with strength will pave

~   **Addendum**   ~

Many times when I was ill in bed
Mom would be my nurse love said

Her love was unconditional and focused
No plague could get me not even locust

Life was tough, but I felt secure
Mom's love was total and clear

Discipline too but now seen dim
Popcorn strings helped the tree trim

Good food and plenty to eat
We had switched to whole wheat

Our music to mom's ears sounded sweet
Spring was awesome with birds and tweet

Gifts oft homemade and sewing all night
On my childhood, selfishness shines new light

Heating with wood and drying clothes by its side
Women from this method today would hide

S and *h* green stamps and coupons galore
Her saving technique allowed us to have more

Sunday was God's day, food already prepared
Even chocolate cake ready and served in layered

Thank you, Mom, for all that you lovingly did
Trouble and hot food both got your lid

Roasts, cookies, cakes, and sandwiches of cheese
Lord, keep these memories fresh, please, please

Now that I'm a parent my job is never done
Mom's hard work, for sure, has my heart won

Memories of Mom are in a room with open door
I swing the door open wide because my mom I adore

Written on occasion of remembering my precious Mother who gave her all for her family and her Lord. She exemplified climbing successfully on the mountain of life. Her legacy is thorough and is grandly memorialized in the quest to do God's will by giving to others so selflessly. My only regret in life is that I would like to have done more to make her life a little easier. I'll see her again in the heavenly realm, but until then, I'll always hear her singing, "Constantly Abiding".

Let It Happen

Test over and waiting now
Before thee, Lord, I bow

What I want is to pass
My future car is filled with gas

What does future hold, I say
I lie now on your tray

Confidence and wisdom don't leave
I seek the reward so to cleave

Waiting, yes, there is no choice
Praises offered with my voice

Choose my candle to light
Flame burns with all my might

⌐ ⌐ ⌐ ⌐ ⌐ ⌐ ⌐ ⌐ ⌐ ⌐ ⌐

Written on occasion of Jonathan suffering through the stress of waiting for
paramedic test results.

⌐ ⌐ ⌐ ⌐ ⌐ ⌐ ⌐ ⌐ ⌐ ⌐ ⌐

Something is Different Around Here

Two and months and growing fast
I sail my ship at full-blown mast

Mom's excitement about a baby
I wonder about this lil' pink sadie

Something is different in the air
Mom's tummy has something in there

Ba-bee ba-bee, that's what I say
Wonder how long it will stay

I have my stuff, and it is mine
A ba-bee a sister she'll even dine

I know the ropes, and I'm big now
During orientation I'll show you how

Share and sorry and sweet are good
Sometimes I act just like I should

Just for the record, I shan't get too tired
I get out of sorts and moody, I'm mired

My car seat has room for only me
I advise two car seats and no fee

Mom, you work so hard getting me out
Sometimes Lauren will take time to pout

I'll work with dad but wait, wait
I'll always close the safety gate

Dad needs me to do many things
Our horseshoe's game will have rings

I'm almost a man now, but you'll see
I'll show you my stuff when I am three

This little sister, just what is the score?
Will there be crying behind her door?

When dressing me, please think and think
I need tough clothes and, yes, no pink

I say cool man and also wow
My grandpa and I speak growl

I'm quiet now with no guile or greed
Engrossed deeply in book to read

So much to learn about this sis
Feelings and hugs and a little kiss

In drama of life, I have a part
I'm first in line in your heart

Love is equal and never thin
Love cleans and then we win

Different but I like it for sure, er
When do I say I'm your brother

This family of ours is really strong
Can we make God loves us our song

When little Lauren arrives no more riddle
I'll just be me, playing second fiddle

Wow, you'll soon each have a pal
Dad and I and Mom and little gal

Think I'm ready, the change will shock
I'll be the proudest brother on any block

Something's different but no game
Your love for me will never wane

Spotlight or shadow it's okay with me
I'm one fourth of our precious family

⌐ ⌐ ⌐ ⌐ ⌐ ⌐ ⌐ ⌐ ⌐ ⌐ ⌐

Written on occasion of my pal Logan while he is waiting for his little sister
to debut. All the differences and adjustments will be revealed as part of
God's plan as He looks down with love.

⌐ ⌐ ⌐ ⌐ ⌐ ⌐ ⌐ ⌐ ⌐ ⌐ ⌐

Nordstrom Castle

It's there and has tree outside back
This castle will have no lack

The perfect timing and the prayers
It is of God with all the layers

The pluses make the minuses fade
Excitedly through the thoughts, I wade

Warm family love will pervade
Yes, Lord, this you have made

Bind us together in this castle
Being here is much less hassle

Momma and babies in this nest
Daddy brings home his very best

Daddy arrives to cheering squad
Challenges and victories to laud

Children older now and have rules
Cherished as precious jewels

The castle has abundant toys
Brother and sister shout joys

Prayers and hugs and kisses good night
Peace and calm and ner a fright

Kitchen symphony of awesome smell
Mom and Dad on couch to quell

Quietness now in every space
O Lord, what amazing grace

Tomorrow will be a busy day
For now, in my arms, just stay

~ ~ ~ ~ ~ ~ ~ ~ ~ ~ ~

Written on occasion of thinking about Jon and Korie and Logan and Lauren in their happy home in Richmond, Virginia.

~ ~ ~ ~ ~ ~ ~ ~ ~ ~ ~

Teacher, I Know the Answer

God gave you to me and my heart speaks
Sip slowly on that tea—I see no leaks

The state couldn't limit your love and prayer
Silent prayers for each student—louder, don't dare

The light of your love will now and forever shine
In time, these little angels will give their sign

Here is Bobbi, the love of my life
Our marriage has very little strife

Retirement doesn't really seem real
Sleeping in—oh yes, what a deal

Thank you is a token for all the loving sacrifice
All those students and some had head lice

So many years and each a joy
Now teach your awesome grand girls and grand boy

Anticipation of retirement is bittersweet, I'm sure
No commute and sleeping in carry much allure

Your heart would break for kids from dysfunction
They bounced between parents and a junction

Remember the crayons, crisp paper, and colored tables
Kids knew where to sit because there were cute labels

Each day, their heads were filled with something new
At the end of each day, it was obvious that they grew

Parents were traumatized, sending their precious to school
Soon they were confident that Mrs. Nordstrom had rule

A favorite time was when students would read aloud
They smiled as they read challenging words and were proud

Music was such a special time—they would sing from heart
At the same time, they were singing they read from a chart

It was as if you were the little red hen and they the chicks
Here a squabble, there a need—everything did have a fix

Now they have graduated, and of course, they'll miss you
Some things will stay in the past—art of glitter and glue

Sun Valley now has a kindergarten sunset at year's end
Wondering what will happen to each as sunrises bend

Some say life is a race and stay in until the end endure
With what you gave, hopefully, life will become adventure

My Hall of Famer, you thoughtfully lock door and hold key
You are filled with so many memories and feel no glee

You look over shoulder one more time as car leaves grounds
You are happy and sad and, for a while, no leaps and bounds

Everything you taught rode high with love on the wave
Everyone admired your professional style and all you gave

If walls could talk, they would joyously tell your laurels
Window of future reveals achievers once your boys and girls

Time to renew after giving so much for so long
Locked in their memory is school underlined with song

Special and precious are two ingredients that are nice
They confirm you are made of lots of sugar and spice

You used the blue swivel chair that spun and rolled
The classroom functioned well as you quietly strolled

Most nonteachers would crave for quick relief
After one-half hour of students—good grief

There was a routine, and students knew the score
You were the key that made their search engines roar

Take another sip of tea and don't let any regret
Enter your mind and on your windowsill set

Let your heart glow knowing you set their pace
They will continue to build knowledge and social grace

Love and respect early became yours as their teacher
You touched their game of life not just from a bleacher

Once upon a time, you faced your first class—oh wow
Don't smile before Christmas, that's control and how

Students tried to please you in so many little ways
Some were troubled and brought an angry life maze

Some were always ready to move ten minutes before bell
They couldn't wait to run and jump and give a good yell

For some, it'll be climbing the ladder, others will go slide
You pray, they'll all keep climbing and have peace abide

The torch is passed to another able leader
The depth of your light is not for yard or meter

Your light has shined over the texture of young lives
The treads of love and confidence in them survives

~ ~ ~ ~ ~ ~ ~ ~ ~ ~ ~

Written on occasion of my bride of thirty-six years retiring from service to students in the San Rafael School District. It has been said that to teach, you must do it with everything you can muster and, if necessary, use words. All your students learned of your love for them just by being around you. Thank you, my darling wife, for all the years of sacrificial giving and all the miles of commute. I cherish you and am honored to call you my awesome wife and mother of two beautiful and special and precious children. Thanks, Bobbi, for all the nurturing you did and the happiness you brought to so many students and their parents.

~ ~ ~ ~ ~ ~ ~ ~ ~ ~ ~

Billiam

Billiam or William—same a name
Whichever one means the same

Do you will to bill or bill to will?
Do you till the will or bill the till?

Are you bill, or are you will—which?
Did I bill or will I will to just itch?

Will I am or bill I am—I will to be bill
Call me a name, but I will not be shrill

Willbilliam is a good solution, yes
I'll know who I am without a guess

Williamabilliam has a bounce and ring
Too long for some people to jing

Puff chest out and hold head up high
I am Williamabilliam and don't ask why

Will I have a bill with ner a frill
A frill on the bill I will to sir Nill

An award is given to that guy Bill
But Will-i-am thinks it is his—oh, big dill

Will can't you chill when Bill gets it?
Will, close your bill and justly sit

Will's bill is not overdue—this or that
Williamabilliam pulls money from hat

Will's not Billie, and Billie's not Willie
Just call me Bill and don't be so silly

Nillie calls him Willie, but who's to blame?
Valentine said Willie-n-Nillie—Great Dane

So Billie ate his bread and chilli—Willienillie
Bread and chilli on his face—milk so spilly

"Billiam, come up here!" teacher said cloudily
I will to bill your parents—this is so maudly

I accept the blame—in corner, I'll sit still
Billiam felt betrayed—no help from Will

Stay after school and take this quill
Write your real name—Bill or is it Will?

Page had one name—it was just brother
The family loves me—they want no other

All these other names, please spare us
Billiam or William—same to my Clare-us

Happy now I'll start to sing "My Bonnie"
Join me, please, sis, your name is Con-knee

I'm sure that I'm not sure what name is Pom
When I do find out, I'll tell my brother Tom

Written on occasion of thinking about my brother Bill as he gets ready for
heart surgery. He'll be fine 'cause he has a tough spine. After the surgery, he
can practice his recline. Recliner is ready, tea is on the stand, sip it slowly
while holding in your hand.

Fix Your Eyes

When on the gurney and rolling
I follow for a time strolling

My three-month son, I love you
We are in this through and through

I stop as they say turn here
They go through the doors with my dear

One thing I'll remember these days
He looked at me—a fixed gaze

He didn't look away at all
He kept looking at me in hall

I remember his eyes still
Through my look—my love to fill

Thanks, Lord, for this fixed gaze shared
I'm so glad this wasn't spared

I turned and held my husband close
His love was a needed dose

The waiting room was our new home
It was clean—fabric and chrome

Little man, fix eyes on this
Our love for you has not tricks

We'll fix our eyes on Jesus—he knows
Moment by moment, his love grows

Rest now and forget surgery days
Thrill me when you awake—fix my eyes

~   ~   ~   ~   ~   ~   ~   ~   ~   ~   ~

Written on occasion of hearing Karen say to us that lil' J.T. had fixed his gaze on her, and it was a very empowering moment. A man just doesn't begin to understand the powerful relationship a mother has for her children. Karen, you are an awesome mom, and I believe your love for J.T. helped him heal and recover quickly. Karen and Jordan, our hearts beat as one for you and J.T. Our prayers were nonstop. Lord, continue to bless our precious little J.T. and his big sister Taryl. Rest now and forget surgery days.

~   ~   ~   ~   ~   ~   ~   ~   ~   ~   ~

Why, Yes, It's Me—I'm Really Three

I'm glad you are here to celebrate
If frozen, we could on pond—skate

I'll only be three for one year
You know, I hold childhood so dear

No more crawling—I stand and walk
I take turns on phone—to talk

Put on some music, and I'll dance
Maybe my stickpony, and I will prance

I've learned to be thankful—and pray
God has blessed me—even this day

I have gramps and grammas and more
Aunts and uncs and cousins galore

I have a bootiful bedroom with view
I love my books—either old or new

Mom and Dad have reduced my strife
This home is best one of my whole life

I cook and serve and even use a broom
My kitchen and utensils are in my room

I'm always in a happy, happy state
When I see Daddy driving in gate

Mom and I are pals—I copy much
Everywhere I look is her touch

It's special with four of us, you see
Three plus one, and you know my J.T.

Looking back, I've grown tro the years
I take in stride what used to be tears

I love to imagine and just dream
Imaginary things are real, it does seem

I can run and jump and climb so quick
I play with Cole—I kick the stick

My makeup consists of lip glosses
My lips shine, and my hair likes tosses

Traveled thirty-six months to get where I am
I take lessons on how to be a ham

Mom and Dad say to bed, to rest, and read
After awhile Mr. Sandman takes the lead

I bask now in the joy of you being here
All my life, I've said you are so very dear

I love God and life and family happiness
I've been told I'm a cute young princess

～　～　～　～　～　～　～　～　～　～　～

Written on occasion of Taryl turning three and the party at her bootiful home. Is time going fast and am I making moments last? The answer is yes, and I am so grateful to God that Taryl and I are very close. Happy birthday, lil' darling, and know that Grandpa Tom is here and not just for the cake. You are a blessing to all of us, and it is fun to watch you grow up. When the candles are blown out, I have a prayer for you. Lord, may Taryl always know your joy even when the sun can't be seen and the rain has center stage.

～　～　～　～　～　～　～　～　～　～　～

Friends

Eddy Anvil

Eddy anvil doesn't bother anyone
He is nothing but real fun

He is strong enough to hit
He is in such awesome fit

He takes hit—surviving all
Eddy anvil would never fall

Eddy anvil is solid in stance
He gives many a second chance

Eddy anvil never lets us down
He does his job—never a frown

Many come and many do go
Eddy takes blow after blow

Eddy anvil sees things take shape
He takes part with never a scrape

Eddy takes his hits and does his part
Eddy is tremendous from start

He isn't lauded and cheered
He is never really sneered

He is always there and ready
He is trustworthy and steady

Things can get bent out of shape
Let's just measure it with a tape

When things are straightened out
Makes you want to just shout

Actions speak louder than words
He doesn't ever stand with nerds

Eddy anvil, I appreciate you so
With you around, I really grow

                  ✍   ✍   ✍   ✍   ✍   ✍   ✍   ✍   ✍   ✍   ✍

Written on occasion of remembering Eddy Holcomb, my true friend and
brother in Christ. Eddy gave me an anvil, and I've always deeply appreciated
it. For the longest time, I wouldn't use it because I didn't want to cause marks
on the surface. You can pound on it all you want, and it can't be dented
or scratched. Eddy anvil came into my head because Eddy Holcomb is the
kind of friend that is there for you and is steady and actually helps get things
straightened out. His lovely wife, Faye, is one of those people you just so
cherish. When you have friends like Eddy and Faye Holcomb, you don't
need to look for any more. There are many differences between Eddy anvil
and Eddy Holcomb, but the biggest one is that Eddy Holcomb has deep
love for his Savior and all those around him. And Eddy Holcomb is a very
giving person. That's how I got Eddy anvil. No no no no no no, Eddy, I
am not saying you are hardheaded. Everyone smiles. We leave this scene as
you can hear the tapping of small hammers on copper on the anvil as one
or both of my grandson's are learning how to shape metal. Hey, boys, it's
getting dark. Time for dinner. Later, I'm going to call Eddy and tell him
how much fun you had on Eddy anvil.

                  ✍   ✍   ✍   ✍   ✍   ✍   ✍   ✍   ✍   ✍   ✍

Charlie Concrete

This guy knows his stuff—trust me
Stairs or patio—he bends his knee

Early morn until late at night
Your driveway will be done right

Concrete truck is running behind
Just part of Charlie's daily grind

Graded and compacted ground ready
Concrete pours out just so steady

Rebar sits on the douby little tops
Charlie works hard until he drops

Come back next day—pull forms, yes
All cleaned up and what next—guess

A check a check a check, oh do, please
Give me my check and don't ever tease

All customers pleased with Charlie's job
First, the concrete then we can hobnob

Charlie's custom concrete—call when can
When others fail, Charlie will stand man

⌁   ⌁   ⌁   ⌁   ⌁   ⌁   ⌁   ⌁   ⌁   ⌁

Written on occasion of thinking of my awesome friend Charlie Leon
Williams III—hard working and a faithful father and husband. When he
pulls up to the job with truck and Bobcat, you know something good is going
to happen. Sometimes his wife, Jan, calls, and you will always hear a happy,
loving comment or two from Charlie. This guy is the best. We leave this scene
with Charlie and Jason cleaning their tools and loading them in the truck.
Charlie calls Jan and lets her know that he'll be on time. Jan says, "Hold
on—Lilly wants to talk to you." This grandchild stole his heart years ago.

⌁   ⌁   ⌁   ⌁   ⌁   ⌁   ⌁   ⌁   ⌁   ⌁

Maggie's

There is a cafe on freeway close
Food and conversation—good dose

Burgers, salads, tuna, and toast
This food one can really boast

Feeling down, need some cheer
Come to Maggies, health is here

Ken greets you as you walk in
Eat something before you spin

Shannon and Sandra take orders, yes
So many choices but don't guess

Is your stomach little (er) than eye
Please save room for great pie

Marilyn Monroe adorns walls up high
Some guys look at her and sigh

On a freezing day, sit near grill
You won't be far from cash till

Come back soon, you we'll miss
Eating here is such great bliss

~ ~ ~ ~ ~ ~ ~ ~ ~ ~ ~

Written on occasion of thinking about my favorite cafe. It's a genuine place with awesome people and scrumptious food. Come on in and get to know some of the locals. You know, those people that have paid taxes all these years and who still can enjoy a good laugh. Those same folks are seriously patriotic and, lest I forget, quite opinionated. Thanks to Ken, Sandy, Shannon, JJ, John, Peter, and Steve—great people who care about this place. We leave this scene with the owner Ken locking the door after another long day.

~ ~ ~ ~ ~ ~ ~ ~ ~ ~ ~

Personify Me

My name is Katy and a dog
What I did could clog a log

Write it all down to the letter
Sorry, I ripped your sweater

I wasn't human but had ears
Tried to be there during tears

I tried not to be in the way
I tried to please in every way

Wasn't human but needed space
Knew your moods from your face

Memories accrued to very high
I never refused or wondered why

I had a problem of getting out
Returned after hearing a shout

Personify me and add some glee
I was really part of the fun family

Whatever you threw, I'd try to catch
How did I know you wanted fetch

Not human, but we walked and walked
Always thirsty—but never squawked

Not human but superdog guard at night
No intruder could withstand my bite

Personify me, and if I could really talk
I'd say, "Obey the Lord and give him the chalk"

Personify me, and if I could tell much
I loved your heartfelt, loving touch

Personify me and listen to my bark
You knew me even in the cold dark

Personify me and look in my eyes
You will succeed after those tries

Personify me, and I jump and run
I always liked being your companion

I'm gone now—yes, all my parts
Do I still live in your hearts?

Written on occasion of my precious friends, the Carsleys, losing their dog in an accident. Made me think about my own childhood dog and all the times we hung out together. This poem was meant to encourage and uplift. One awesome blessing is to be able to recount all the events that were shared together. A scrapbook with the timeline of memories often helps preserve the intense affection for a companion dog. Lord, bless the Carsleys and help them to know the depth of their church family's love for them. Help them also to know that their participation in the work of the Lord is never taken for granted at this moment, Lord. Hold them in the hollow of your hand that their deep capacity to show love is a steadying force in our midst. Lord, make this verse come alive to them in a new way. Nehemiah 8:10 says, "The joy of the Lord is my strength." Jeff, Emy, Ted, and Jack—God bless you richly.

Joyous Sunami

Shopping nearly over and yet
I really don't know what to get

Cash is great, nobody will burn
No lineup for a return

One size fits all and no reject
Don't lose your wallet from neglect

Cinnamon fills the air at home
Tree looks happy with colorful domes

Heart and hearth do proclaim
God's blessings fall like rain

Sunami floods my being with joy
God, use me in your will and employ

Family and friends gather inside
Christmas meal and then a hayride

A toast to the goodness and strength of God
Thankful for rich love and thorough rod

Lots of talk about who's wrapped enough
Young boys in the cold think they are tough

We are in a living Kinkade
Heaven our family has made

Over hill and through vale
Tipping slightly into the swale

Singing joyfully and sipping cider
Turning and jostling holding tighter

There's the gristmill and the store
Soon we will see much more

The ride has slack and lurch
We turn the corner and see the church

Pastor Don and wife, Jewell, at the door
Hugs and praises and, yes, tell me more

Inside the woodstove, its heat is serving
In the kitchen, not a goodie is burning

Coffee, pumpkin pie, and sticky buns
The butter on top down the side now runs

Reaching out to others in this church's mission
On Sunday, no one real serious is out fishin'

The adorned altar has seen many a reunion
Souls have met Christ and now sweet communion

Pastor Don gives a challenge from God's Word
Jesus's peace is different from the dove bird

Service has ended outside in the black sky
Stars remind us we're the apple of God's eye

Two large sleighs with each having four horses
Cold toes and cold noses, warm blood have their courses

Singing God's carols and from the cold bundling
Such a good time you never hear word of grumbling

Each horse has bells that announce our coming
Harmony and beat is kept by the deacon's strumming

Christmas is wonderful, glad Jesus left the stall
For some people, Jesus only fits in the mall

Gifts and giving makeup their belief
From sin and punishment, Christ gives relief

Snow and crystal wind make faces feel raw
This winter Kinkade will soon be in thaw

People, get out at home from this taxi
Happy to be home and entering by latch and key

Soon the deacon and four horses alone
Go to the barn a little weary, a little worn

Horses are now free of leads and straps
Babies now going to sleep in fathers' laps

Thank you, Lord, for this Kinkade, that is true
It can never grow old, only just seem new

Christ Jesus, you suffered cut and lesion
Jesus, I love you, the reason for the season

～   ～   ～   ～   ～   ～   ～   ～   ～   ～   ～

Written on occasion of Christmas Eve '05 for all who now love or want to
have God's love and plan for their life, God bless you and give to you His love.

～   ～   ～   ～   ～   ～   ～   ～   ～   ～   ～

Slingshot Memories

No TV and no Tevo gun
But we learned to run

Hard work but eve time
Mom's bread and apple jime

Dad's clever in his spare time
Memories now tickle my spine

Vermin traps, whistles, and slingshots
We all had 'em—from biggest to tots

Dad would hunt like stealthy stork
Finding tree with a perfect fork!

Carving knife, leather, and stretch
Slingshot missile hard to ever catch

Dad's slingshots were strong and true
Dad would whittle, and mom turned stew

Times were special—not now in style
Might find it now by turning TV dial

Dad would share wisdom by that fire
Honesty travels—breakdowns fit a liar

Messages came sometimes with no word
He was strong but gentle—with a bird

His slingshot fired high and far
His targets would show a mar

He must have shot some really hard
Years later, they land in my yard

Slingshot words of wisdom guide me
Years later, I hear them so clearly

Mom would call and to house we'd run
Slingshots helped us have lots of fun

Dad gave me his slingshot from ago
It causes me to remember to and fro

He told me I'd have Goliaths just ahead
Faith and trust would see them dead

Slingshot is worn and shiny—and a split
Dad, let's go back to that ole fire and sit

Mom, would you pass me some of the grit?
Heading for school with scarf and mit

Memories are like chocolate on silver tray
If I could go back there, I'd want to stay

Slingshot lessons, and I have learned some
One of your gifts was always loving Mom

Walk with me and talk of those old times
Jesus's love is the true tie that really binds

The slingshot, my companion—fair or jarred
Let me shoot a Goliath and never be barred

The world can be dark and really quite cold
With the Lord and slingshot, you'll be bold

Written on occasion of seeing Jewel Smith's father's slingshot and touching it. I was honored to see an artifact of Jewell's childhood because of the deep love she has for her parents. May it never be forgotten what your dad and mom have done for you. When Goliaths see that slingshot, they tremble and try to outrun the stone of judgment. God bless.

Gristing Along

Springtime was special and full
Warmth surrounded and time to mull

Water glistened as the large wheel turned
Gristmill now grinding, and people learned

Corn would be ground fine, medium, or coarse
Happy shouting, no voice would get hoarse

Heart joyful as down the road to the mill
Listening to springtime as I oft stood still

Owners of the mill greeted me as a kin
From the window, the large stones did spin

On tiptoes, I placed my order with glee
A little fine, medium, and coarse all three

Grandma would add water too coarse for hens
Happy and clucking as they blinked their lens

Ground corn came from the power of the wheel
Too bad today all we have to do is open a seal

Memories are precious tho wheel now has rust
Thinking about it can make me smell corn dust

Walking back home with bags in hand
I was important and breezes fanned

Peaceful and full of country's grace and charm
People round came with corn from the farm

Corn smelled and tasted good as Momma fixed it
Corn bread or grits going long with brisket

Fresh corn on cob, I tried braiding the silk
We ate well and had pie with cold milk

Gristmill was part of a life that had no care
Thought 'bout riding the wheel but did not dare

Life seemed happier when those stones did spin
Some were well-off and for some it was thin

Bags I delivered were a product of God's love
Rewarded by thank-you and hug as of dove

Going to the grist was never a chore
Felt secure and happy and could use more

Winter chill and leaves falling in the frisk
O Lord, thank you for memories of the grist

~   ~   ~   ~   ~   ~   ~   ~   ~   ~   ~

Written on occasion of hearing memories of the grist from our precious
sister Jewel Smith. Jewel and Don are close kin to us even tho' we have a
different last name.

~   ~   ~   ~   ~   ~   ~   ~   ~   ~   ~

Demo Dave

Someone needs their house torn down
Demo Dave arrives with cat and sound

Demo Dave's cat will move and crunch
This cat eats a house way before lunch

The big bucket opens and crunches closed
Sidekick Neal hits the dust with his hose

Soon the house is down and demo Dave grinds
Debris gets crunched—even the blinds

Big trucks back in—hungry for a load
Now the crunched house goes down road

Load by load the pile is showing less
Doesn't take long to clean up this mess

Concrete and metal to recycle must go
Debris is all gone and overnight can't grow

Sidekick Neal checks for anything on edges
Wind may have blown something in hedges

The big cat stops making a big roar
Just sits and purrs and waits for more

Battle is won between big cat and big house
Everyone knew who'd win—cat is no mouse

Sidekick Neal picks up tools and hose in reel
Neighbor hopes the big cat loved its meal

Big cat gets greased, and demo Dave checks fuel
Old-timer says in the '40s—owner had a mule

The lot is now clean and level and clear
Hard to believe a house was once here

The big cat is sleeping with its engine off
Just sits there, and you'll not hear a cough

Demo Dave says to Neal—cat has had a munch
Sure am hungry—let's go to Maggies for lunch

Green Ford turns corner and goes out of sight
"Hard work," says Dave, "getting paid makes it right"

Afternoon shadows stretch over length and girth
Demo Dave and Neal give lot back to mother earth

⌀ ⌀ ⌀ ⌀ ⌀ ⌀ ⌀ ⌀ ⌀ ⌀ ⌀

Written on occasion of thinking back on the process of a house demolition.
Some people have never seen it happen, and they wouldn't know how. They just
stand with eyes wide open and say a hearty wow. Written by 'ol Bobcat Tom.

⌀ ⌀ ⌀ ⌀ ⌀ ⌀ ⌀ ⌀ ⌀ ⌀ ⌀

Smoke Signal

A terrorist killed this lad's beloved dad
Something like this makes me soulfully sad

Terrorist died too—but what price is paid?
Precious life had no meaning—just a fade

I love you, Dad, imprinted on his heart
You loved me too, Dad, from the start

The 9/11 is a day to remember all firefighters—yes
They passionately save lives—others to bless

You'd be proud of me, Dad, started something new
My colors don't run, Dad, the red, white, and blue

This imaginary smoke signal goes up now
I think about you, Dad, my head does bow

Dad, God will help me be a real man just like you
Dad, you were so dedicated, faithful, and true

I'm man of the house now—mom cries a lot
I hold her tightly, and my tears well up and drop

I'll see you in heaven, Dad, and until then
I'll be strong and carry on—I know I really can

Yes, I am a Geraghty and proud heritage, I have
The pain will always be there—you give me salve

We used to walk hand in hand to the store
Now I try filling your shoes—but what a chore

~   ~   ~   ~   ~   ~   ~   ~   ~   ~   ~

Written on occasion of appreciating Connor Geraghty and the deep love
he has for his dad and mom. I pray for him and would love to meet him
someday. This poem was meant to encourage him and tell him that he is not
alone. I agree with him that 911 should be National Firefighters' Day.

~   ~   ~   ~   ~   ~   ~   ~   ~   ~   ~

Mortician's Morning

This is your day, Lord, truly, yes
I want to give all not less

My work is different from most folks
I deal with bodies and no jokes

I'll never run out of clients to see
Their journey hellish or heavenly

Tools familiar, I know what to do
Bodies won't sit up and say boo

All dressed up and one place to go
In the ground under rain, sun, or snow

Blessed be the truthful fact
In the ground, we are not intact

Our spirit left at point of death
Let's not stand around all bereft

When the spirit left to be with the Lord
Left for others is the two-edged sword

As the morning, sun aids the embalming process
Your love for me is so very real—no need to guess

I'm used to it now, Lord, the bodies don't move
You, I, and this body as if in a small cove

Today, again, lots of serious thought
All t's have been crossed, every i has a dot

Their tasks over on earth nothing more to wrought
Wonder if they spent time for Jesus sought

The body now ready, and it's half past nine
All prep done and no more paper to sign

The family gathers and views my work
Viewing is good, no sign of a smirk

Readying and preparing and transporting slow
Everyone in traffic seems to respect the show

The hearse carries a message by just one look
The body inside its life from it took

Everyone knows that there's an appointed time
On that day will be a beautiful bell's chime

The Christian secure for eternity will be
Crown of glory and all that is heavenly

Morning almost over now, and I have a hunch
I'll be real busy so I'll have a quick lunch

~ ~ ~ ~ ~ ~ ~ ~ ~ ~ ~

Written on occasion of thinking how different my work is from my friend
Chris' work.

~ ~ ~ ~ ~ ~ ~ ~ ~ ~ ~

It Works

My trust for computers is very low
Good things happen, and I grow

E-mails and www's appear in time
Amazing what you get for a dime

Dennis Keney is such a great friend
When he moved, it was not the end

When you love the Lord with all your heart
True Christian friends will not depart

Computers help—together we stick
Message speed is really, really quick

Best communication is in the deep layer
When we are moved for a friend in prayer

Written on occasion of reconnecting with Dennis Keney and receiving his new email address.

Do You Remember?

The church in Hopland needed a leader
I gave of myself with unbridled meter

God spoke through sermons and thank thee
Usually the message was focused for me

How did you know, Lord, that I cried
Reach this town, reach this town—we tried

There were many trials and challenges we faced
Each had a before, during, and after—prayer laced

My wife and I wept, prayed, and sang
Remember our heart bells truly rang

Sunday after Sunday with you to endure
Lord, you wanted obedience and to be pure

Lord, remember so many victories won
The sin lifted felt like a big heavy ton

I'm facing surgery now those bones to repair
Independence from the yoke of sin, I declare

The Lord knows my need, he answers the best
Not to worry keeps a load off my chest

It's another test, and battles are yours, Lord
Victory in Jesus and the Word is my sword

I want to glorify you, Lord, this is sealed
I pray the doctors say, "Hold it, he is healed"

The VA hospital is ready for me—yes, true
Relief from pain is just long overdue

My needs, my comfort, my body, I put on a shelf
I want to minister to others and forget about self

May I always stand firm with hands out to thee
Seeing your work in lives and Satan to flee

Thank you, Lord, for the privilege of being yours
My spirit lifts, and then with you, it really soars

~ ~ ~ ~ ~ ~ ~ ~ ~ ~ ~

Written on occasion of pastor Don Smith preparing for hip surgery in the VA of San Francisco. We know, Lord, you will pour out blessings and withhold not even a small one. God bless you, Don, and remember the great physician is on duty, and everybody answers to Him. Be encouraged.

~ ~ ~ ~ ~ ~ ~ ~ ~ ~ ~

Adoptable

My new parents—coming soon to Bogotá
I can't wait—my heart is saying rah and rah

Everything new—God blesses from above
Their hearts are overflowing with love

This new family, yes, five in a row
Will sit in church with hearts aglow

Your love, Lord, and timing aren't stopable
You have this plan, yes, we are adoptable

Written on occasion of Jenny as she endures the delay of the adoption.

Wash or Dry, Are You Spry?

Wash or dry, are you spry
Don't let the soap hit an eye

Is machine too small or clothes big?
This laundry thing is not my gig

I keep my shirt carefully tucked in
White briefs now colored in spin

Red ran into white now, what sight
Either buy new or wear this plight

Like socks—said pretty redhead
One white and one bleeder instead

Are there clothes nice and sturdy?
No wrinkles and never get dirty?

Wash or dry, are you spry?
Mud or sud and electricity high

Metal clothing—no rust or crust
Machine and pile—now I really must

⌐ ⌐ ⌐ ⌐ ⌐ ⌐ ⌐ ⌐ ⌐ ⌐ ⌐

Written on occasion of wishing I could purchase a washer and dryer for my
nephew and his wife. Blessings on your wedding and marriage and may all
your problems be little ones.

⌐ ⌐ ⌐ ⌐ ⌐ ⌐ ⌐ ⌐ ⌐ ⌐ ⌐

The Bed Said

What are you doing here now?
Why aren't you up eating chow?

Oh, bed, I'm sick today all over
Soon though, I'll run in clover

Oh, bed, you feel so very good
Normally, I'd be up—I would

Bed, you've always been there
This time I caught a germ in air

I'd rather be up, but I'm not sad
Jesus will help me, be very glad

I thank him even when I feel bad
Helping me is my own loving dad

Written on occasion of talking with Chris Cowan and daughter Kennedy. She was sick in bed and wanted to tell me she is excited about showing me her poems on Sunday. I told her we would write a poem together. She'll never know how much that meant to me. Chris—thanks for being there for your children. When they are older, they won't remember all you've said, but they will remember that you cared and loved.

The Buck Stops Here

The new horse didn't want to slow
Attitude here was ready to show

Loose in saddle—not ready for this
Bucked me off—boulders I did miss

That buck stopped here, and I dared
Wind knocked out of me—'twas spared

Walked to horse, gave me a head toss
It was clear that there was only one boss

There followed groundwork and much
Horse soon obeyed my voice and touch

Remembering my first horse at seventeen
We were inseparable, she was so keen

Many days I would talk to that great horse
When she passed away, I had such remorse

We had been through so much together
She was my horse, and I was her tether

I knew that horse as much as I knew myself
Riding would often improve my mental health

When I rode her, I was away from human stress
I even rode her some times wearing a dress

A girl and her horse in such awesome motion
I knew her so well—even her every notion

I knew it was time—she was going to go
Didn't care that my tears and crying did show

Even though she is gone, her memories fresh
Close my eyes, and I can almost feel her flesh

I learned a lot caring for that great pal
Commitment and some horse sense and val

Pastor Tom and his wife, Bobbi, helped me then
It was so hard to say good-bye to my friend

I felt empty and way out on a limb
My joy seemed to lessen and was dim

We prayed together and asked for strength
We stood at her grave and talked at length

The new horse is different, it's very clear
Old horse had become so near and so dear

We thanked the Lord for the blessings brought
Blessings now memories buried in this spot

Buried but not forgotten—loved you so much
All those hours riding, cleaning, and such

Yes, new horse, I purchased you for a grand
Treat me like the old horse—I demand

It'll take some time to give you my heart
The buck stops here is a very good start

      ~ ~ ~ ~ ~ ~ ~ ~ ~ ~ ~

Written on occasion of talking with our precious friend Rhonda who had
lost her horse she had had for many years. We were there to help her in any
way we could. We prayed with her about this big change in her life. Life is

always going to have big changes, but our reliance on Christ's strength and knowing he deeply cares is our foundation. God bless you, Rhonda, as you think sometimes of your first horse bittersweet event, but we always grow closer to Christ as we put everything in His eternal perspective. Love to you in the name of Jesus. From Tom the Baptist and Bobbi of thirty-eight years.

Hector

Who is this guy doing so much?
He has the multitask touch

He wants every book to sell
They all have a story to tell

He works in the admin sector
Mess up, and he will lecture

Hurry up, send that script now
Sometimes he looks and says wow

Who can tell the hours he keeps?
Sometimes he goes and sleeps

Getting books published is the rage
He says there is one more page

When your book sells, he is in dough
He wants your book to look just so

Workday done—he takes stock
He's last out and turns the lock

Going home is like closing a book
Now at home—coffee and nook

Written on occasion of thinking about all the work that Hector, the publishing guy, must go through to get good books on the market. He also enjoys a good joke, so when we talk on the phone, I always try to tell him one. He doesn't know that I am borderline second personality . . . because sometimes I'm beside myself!

The Sunday Times

Money goals and visions change
Coming back here felt very strange

This is where I attended Sunday school
Mrs. Soberman was a teacher cool

She made every lesson come alive
She never was paid not even a five

Her pay must have been teaching kids
Her prayer was that none would hit skids

I was always impressed with her ways
Always upbeat and praising her craze

Never trained but taught with grace
Made me feel good to see her face

Those Sunday times are back in past
Lessons learned from her will last

I'm back to visit and see the old room
Building condemned torn down in June

Looked through window and just thought
Where would I be without what she taught?

Mrs. Soberman, you are a heroine to me
You really helped me—Jesus to see

Your husband was killed in a distant war
You were so faithful I just wanted more

You always brought milk and cookies
You grew us up in the Lord—from rookies

Purity of your service—and love of Christ
God's spirit guided you, and I was enticed

I came from the orphanage across town
You sidetracked me from being a clown

Remember family pictures on the flannel board
My mom died, and my dad drove off in a Ford

My life at the orphanage was pretty rough
I reacted when anyone gave me any guff

There was peace in my heart in your class
It never occurred to me to give you sass

I cried many times that no one adopted me
You said God adopted me, and I'm family

I ached for love and accepted Christ soon
Your love and teaching gave me a boon

I was transferred, but you kept in touch
Your letters were cherished so very much

You believed in me, I didn't know it then
You said with Jesus you can succeed—you can

We wrote each month until you passed away
My little girl, she wants to be like you someday

In the orphanage, I cried gallons of tears
Christmastime pain was like many spears

Don't know how you did it, but always a gift
Came to each of your students—what a lift

I hold my wife close as this view strikes me
Because of you I'm on God's loving family tree

~   ~   ~   ~   ~   ~   ~   ~   ~   ~   ~

Written on occasion of remembering that my own father was adopted and
was raised in a loving home. He was very sickly when he was chosen and
became a great man of God.

There are a lot of sickly people in this world that need to know they have been
chosen by Christ, and all they have to do is accept Him as the one who paid
the price for sin-sickness and then be fully adopted into the family of God.

Mrs. Soberman is a fictitious character, but the world is full of people like
her that give so much and yet don't have much of this world's goods. God
always provides for the ones that truly serve Him. Thanks, Mom and Dad
for all your sacrifices that I appreciate more now.

~   ~   ~   ~   ~   ~   ~   ~   ~   ~   ~

Church

Words of Hurt

My church is full of nice folk
What hit my ear was no joke

I was accused of sinning, yes
I tried to hide, my little mess

I don't like someone telling me
The truth for me to really see

Ashamed, I admitted my failing
Behind *forgiveness*, I'm trailing

It was
written down and fact
I was caught and no more tact

I asked if we could talk alone
I felt bad even in each bone

This time, I was caught and how
This time, I decided knees to bow

Forgive me, no power to quit
Let me help, come here and sit

I needed the help, I admit it now
You are there for me as I bow

I'm glad you are my friend forever
You've promised our ties never sever

The words had really hurt me
You helped me while on my knee

With you, I know I need no other
You my sins I know did cover

I feel brand new with power in tank
Lord Jesus, my Savior, you I thank

Written on occasion of remembering when I asked Christ to be my Savior. I wanted to be with Him in heaven instead of being with my enemy at his place. At first, the words hurt when I found out I was a sinner. Wasn't I just as good as the next guy? I was convicted and doomed to hell until I talked with God alone and asked for forgiveness. Now the words don't hurt but serve as a reminder that I most definitely needed to hear them. What really got my attention was that I heard that Jesus died for my sins even when I didn't even care about him, and also he wanted me to accept him and live for him. I was caught by his love for me, and he drew me into himself. Many years later, I still mess up, but Jesus helps clean me up and gives me new desires that come from his heart. We leave this scene with the man helping with a Sunday school class. It's time to close the class, and outside the door, his wife is holding their newborn. You might say that there are actually two newborns, but one is thirty years old.

Street Preacher

Why does he stand in fair or foul?
Why does he say search your soul?

He a fixture now on Saturday morns
Is it too much? Christ wore thorns

Silent prayer and love to whom passes
Some walk by and others show dashes

Church bells peal, "How great Thou art!"
Not even wobbly, he does his part

Matching God's Word with a thirst
If you ask, he'll be well versed

Some curse the Word and the messenger
At the Judgment Day, what vestiture?

Leaving this post, and sky is still blue
Why does he do what he can do?

Next, he'll say hi to Sam, the barber
Then there'll be lunch under arbor

Street preacher, how can we measure?
You giving this highest of all treasure

Others first, it's His glory I seek
My prize is the calling, He doth speak

At home, my wife takes hat and coat
Hands me something a friend has wrote

Burdened now for a very young lad
Stopped to listen with eyes of sad

If he seeks You, he'll not be forsook
Truth abounds in the handout he took

Comforting fire of oakery and hickory
Help me, Lord, with voice of victory

Written on occasion of thinking about the street preaching that Rev. Don Smith does in the towns of N. County. The word never goes out void, and that means that there is victory somewhere in someone because of the efforts. Praise God for all His blessings; but I want one more, and that is a grateful heart, a big thank-you to the voice of victory team that delivers the message of salvation from the hard platform of concrete to hearts that could be of stone. Don't give me a reward because I've already been paid. My humble sacrifice of praise has been laid at His feet in an attempt to do my utmost for His highest love.

The Steep of the Steeple

The steep of the steeple was bothering me
Seemed its disrepair was shaming to Thee

A few dollars and a lot of elbow grease
It now adorns the house of peace

Rust and mold had taken a good strong hold
Being up there with paint took someone bold

Funny how one's perspective changes up there
Balance between footing and just thin air

Rust and mold thoroughly cleaned away
Elements now would not show their sway

I thought about a lot of things on that tower
Thank you, Lord, that no wires give us power

Poles and wires go all around this town
Here power comes from knees on the ground

This lighthouse church sits up here so clear
We survive the storm if we let You steer

These buildings always need so much attention
In our prayers, the repairs are always a mention

One person doing a part that's given to You
Lord, we have confidence You'll make it new

It no longer bothers me it's bright and clean
Satan lost this one, no need for his scene

The tasks are overwhelming, and shall we dare?
Yes, Lord, yes, You are able, and we know You care

We put on Your full armor, the battle is Yours
Victory in Jesus, and then our confidence soars

One steeple, one person, and the job had to be done
May others take on a battle and say it's been won

      ~   ~   ~   ~   ~   ~   ~   ~   ~   ~   ~

Written on occasion of Pastor Chris Cowan having painted the church cross and tower. The reminder is so vivid: if I be lifted up, I will draw all men to Me.

      ~   ~   ~   ~   ~   ~   ~   ~   ~   ~   ~

Key of Yesteryear

It was time for new locks and keys
Robbers could not our value seize

My old key was a companion ready
Let it go now—don't be so petty

You don't understand—this key works
I see it and know a memory lurks

Silently, holding this key helps friend
My memory video plays without end

Thousands of times, this key and lock met
I look back so fast—am I on a jet?

I used this key when my life had a mar
The key to comfort came at the altar

I'll leave this key on my ring for now
May it unlock passion for God—a bow

This key locked your house on Sunday
Unlocked my heart to love anyway

It's just a key, and I do just want to say
It is special to me, Lord, may I not stray

New locks and new keys—on duty now
My old key gives me a boost somehow

The new key and the old—together ride
New key and new memories to abide

One ends a chapter, and one starts new
Old key represents many ways I grew

Old key shows an altar—You took my shame
My heart, your altar—Your love the flame

Written on occasion of Pastor Chris Cowan regretfully discarding his old
church key. Many of us have experienced that feeling in degrees of meaning.
A church key that you've had for years is so different from a key to something
else. The Lord will continue to bless you, Chris, and you work so hard to
open locked hearts to the power, peace, and purpose of the Christian life.
There are keys you can never misplace or lose, and they never grow old—the
keys to heaven.

Nature

Ear Wap

Ear wap, you hurt so much
You don't know a soft touch

There you were still on the wood
I didn't cut you as I should

My ears were almost frozen that morn
Touching them felt like frozen corn

Funny thing as I loaded last piece
Ear wap pressure sure did release

How did you know my ear was there
Ear wap, you whistled through air

You hurt me so bad I won't forget
It won't happen again, you can bet

I know this could have been prevented
The reminder is my ear is temporarily dented

How many times have I been wapped
By things I could have clearly stopped

Things should have been done timely
Instead, they turned out rather slimily

Ear wap, your dismissal, I hail
Hope I don't hit my hammer on my nail

⌐ ⌐ ⌐ ⌐ ⌐ ⌐ ⌐ ⌐ ⌐ ⌐

Written on occasion of remembering the morning I was enjoying loading
firewood and neglected to cut off a four-foot-long skinny branch. That's the
one that snapped up and wapped my very cold ear, and it really stung. So
many times in life, we can let things go until they come back to us and give

us pain. Thank God for forgiveness and mercy when we are hit by our own mistakes. Some are the kind that hurt ourselves, and others are hurts that can last a lifetime. Like the guy who couldn't control his behavior in front of his children and later in life felt the wap of loneliness because his children didn't want anything to do with him . . . Lord, right now I ask you to help me learn from my wapping mistakes and to be a better servant of yours.

Falling for Me

Grandpa and I sat in morn'n cold
Time together was better than gold

Making memories together with a book
Finished reading and cuddled in our nook

Oak tree leaves began to fall
From the patio, tree looked so tall

Leaves fell in groups to the ground
Watched and thrilled at orange and brown

Two chums sitting, watching God's show
Sun glistened on water droplets aglow

Grandpa, the leaves are taking their turn
That's something in school we learn

Leaves stopped falling for a spell
When they fall again, who can tell?

The scene was beautiful and so cool
Grandpa, let's make a good rule

When the next leaf falls, we'll go in
Leaves do fall softer than sound of pin

Funny thing happened, no leaves fell
Waiting and waiting, a leaf we did tell

I jumped up and blew at the tree
Hoping a leaf would fall just for me

Looking high in the tree for the next
To see it float to its earthly rest

Suddenly, the lowest leaf dropped
Our waiting now had stopped

We laughed, and both agreed to go in
Poppa and I, a new adventure to begin

Written on occasion of sitting together with Taryl on the back patio with all of nature unfolding before us—unusual how all the other leaves had been falling from up in the tree, and the last one we watched fell from the lowest branch. Reminds me of the times we miss the blessings closest to us because we are looking for the highest and mightiest, and the grandiose. The experiences we have that are close to us are the ones to pin up on the memory board of our hearts. Wish now that I had tried to find that leaf as a reminder to be true to those people and events closest to me. God bless, America, and God bless you.

My Turf

I found some land
Beaut view but too much sand

Another place was just too good
Steam now under the hood

I cooled down and so did car
What price, 'twas ready for jar

$100 a month and no other fees
Ten years, and its yours, if you please

$120,000 for this big beaut spread
Yes, son, are you spinning in the head?

We prayed someone of passion would appear
Turned a lot of people down 'til you dear

You are right, and what a match
Here is the key to the old latch

I'll take it. I'll take it full of deep joy
"We'll visit you once a year," said Moie

Bless you, son, dear
Bless you, Mama Moie and Papa Grear

Moie and Greer ride away in their Cadillac and wave as they turn by the
stone bridge. The young man didn't know that they owned about half the
valley and had several homes dotting through the mountains. He unlocks
the door and smells some beef stew that Moie had cooked for him. The
moon shone through the curtains as he lay back on the old couch.

~   ~   ~   ~   ~   ~   ~   ~   ~   ~   ~

Written on occasion of thinking about my nephew Jon Calvin Nordstrom,
and his purchase of rural property.

~   ~   ~   ~   ~   ~   ~   ~   ~   ~   ~

Cake of la Fruit

A friend sends me one
Wrapped so beautifully, it's fun

Many colors packed so dense
Really affects my taste sense

You really like 'em or you hate 'em
Cake of la fruit you are a gem

Hot coffee and a slice of la fruit
No complaints will I begin to toot

Winter blasts hit my cabin I adore
Cake of la fruit, you are no chore

I savor each taste, add coffee down
Want some, then gather all around

Some folks think cake of la fruit a flop
At Christmas, they use it as a doorstop

Such dishonor to this culinary star
Eat it at home or when in your autocar

Little table by the warmth of the stove
What is that on plate—oh, treasure trove

Cake of la fruit sits invitingly there
Why do I sit here and carry on a stare?

Sliced to perfection—not thick or too thin
Cake of la fruit and my coffee, is it sin?

Rich and sweet and dense besides
Say it's ready, and I'll take big strides

Many are mailed, and many are shipped
Some say they wish they had been skipped

Too bad they are missing out on this cake
For them is something else to bake

The snow piles deep, and some are cooking
Cake of la fruit—center stage booking

Sing the carols and your instrument toot
I'll sit here and listen and eat cake of la fruit

Written on occasion of remembering my friend Dennis Keney sending us a
fruitcake each year. It is an acquired taste, and man, it is really good. Fruitcake
has a bad rep from many that haven't taken the time to enjoy it. No, it wasn't
made by the devil. Slide your chair closer to the warm fire and listen to the
crackle of the wood. Try a small piece as you know you should. Then if you
do or if you refuse, we still can enumerate the blessings of the Lord. Come
here, my grandchildren, and crawl up on Grandpa's leg. A story is brewing.
)To you, it will suit, began when I ate some cake of la fruit.)

Pressure of Blood

That ole heart pumps the blood
Works so well without a sud

Oxygen is picked up in the lungs
Those busy red cells go the rungs

White cells stay on duty 24/7
Like the bread with the leaven

Red cells die and replenish
Healthy cells are a good wish

Couch potatoes simmer in skin
Runners race not to really win

High pressure or very, very low
Neither one is good for show

Too much weight and use of salt
Aren't good with a choc malt

Good pressure comes to the fit
Exercise now—show true grit

Some care not about their days
Pushing daisies is their gaze

Exercise now, and yes, it shows
Been a while since you saw toes

Move now in a committed decree
Hey, potato, turn off the TV

My heart beats both day and night
Oh, Lord, I'll keep it working right

Some folks run or do the bamba
yourself, drink juice of jamba

～　～　～　～　～　～　～　～　～　～　～

Written on occasion of taking my blood pressure with my home kit, praising
God for that part of me that beats continually in spite of the amount of sleep
or what I eat. This is a temple of the Holy Spirit, and I want to keep it fit for
God's service. Oh yes, Thanks, Lord, for getting me home alive from Vietnam
and also for seeing to it that I was cured of prostrate cancer. Those are joy
builders and joy is the opposite of stress. Stress and high blood pressure are
chums that hang out together. God bless you richly and thankfully.

～　～　～　～　～　～　～　～　～　～　～

Patriotism

Name on Wall

Honey, why is your name on the wall?
I like it 'cause I am good and tall

Who will clean it off today?
But I want it to just stay

We have rules, walls stay clean
Clean it now, this I really mean

If removed, my name won't show
Proud of my name, do you know?

A picture of it and then a frame
Someday, will I gain any fame

Many will see your name, son
Dedication for the prize you won

What should I be, my mom?
A leader son, not a pon

Want to marry and have kids
They'll play with pots, pans, and lids

Will I know when I am in love?
It's when you hug and not shove

Later, as the Mom holds a tearstained picture of her little boy's name on the kitchen wall—she chokes and sobs and falls to her knees. She sobs out loud and says, "Yes, son, your name is on the wall where everyone who shows their respects can see it. Oh son, I am so glad I didn't blow up at you for writing on the wall 'cause now I cherish this little picture and the precious memories." She cries and speaks to this boy whose name is still on the wall as loved ones hold her as they too sit on their knees. Husband and father speaks gently when he feels it is time for them to begin leaving—a hint of winter is felt in the air. She is carefully lifted to her feet and sobbingly whispers, "Let me touch him. Let me touch him." Her deft fingers trace each letter of his name as tears cascade down her face.

God bless you, son. I'll see you soon in heaven. Jesus saves.

We leave this scene as the brother-in-law approaches with a lawn chair and a bottle of water. She struggles to get a swallow down between sobs. She sits in the lawn chair as the husband and brother-in-law carry her to the car. A granddaughter from her daughter walks up and says that "Jesus will help you grandma."

"Oh honey, you shouldn't see your grandma crying so much."

"It's okay grandma. I am sad too, and you teach me more about real love." The two cars of family drive to Grandma's house so she won't be alone. This traveling display of the Vietnam wall is a powerful reminder to all who view it of the dedication of those who gave it all. As they made their payment toward what isn't free—our liberty—grandma rocks on the back porch until wee hours of the morning, thanking God for the strength it took to go to the wall. The grandkids didn't mean that Grandma would be all alone. They knew Grandpa was here too. They just knew that he needed help. He too was grieving. He was actually the last one to turn from the wall. Before he did, he saluted his son's name as if his son could hear him. He said, "Yes, son, your name will always be on our wall. I loved you then, and I love you now. We'll be together in heaven soon. Thank you for reading this, and yes, God bless, America."

⌐   ⌐   ⌐   ⌐   ⌐   ⌐   ⌐   ⌐   ⌐   ⌐   ⌐

Written on occasion of thinking about the emotional pain that families endure after losing a loved one in war.

⌐   ⌐   ⌐   ⌐   ⌐   ⌐   ⌐   ⌐   ⌐   ⌐   ⌐

Veteran Stops

I love my country, the good ole USA
Now that I'm a vet, I just want to pray

Before I served, I was free of fear
Now the Lord gives joy, it is clear

No TV in my house, violence deeply hurts
No need for anything to bring back alerts

Sounds, smells, and sights bring flashbacks
I was in armored infantry with guns and tracks

Thanks for remembering and seeing what I see
"America, the Beautiful", and freedom is not free

~   ~   ~   ~   ~   ~   ~   ~   ~   ~   ~

Written on occasion of Tom Nordstrom sitting and hearing a helicopter pass overhead. Good memories of choppers. Tom's depth of gratitude cannot be measured, yet he wants to give back a little of what he has received. Thank you, Lord. Yes, thank you, Lord. In dedication to Don Smith who continues to serve. Love ya, brother.

~   ~   ~   ~   ~   ~   ~   ~   ~   ~   ~

Iraqistan

Two places combined but still
Action and death give same chill

Higher calling gives you your push
Guns stop—listen to that hush

Thanks guys for helping the goal
Spreading freedom for every soul

The same sun that gave you light today
Has served us and went over your way

The same wind that blew against us here
Cools you and calms a little of your fear

This Viet vet understands your test
Daily, you try to do your country's best

Moment by moment not your control
Sometimes you walk or lie in a hole

Family and friends say a sincere prayer
They light up the darkness with their care

Trust for each other goes very deep
A letter from home makes heart leap

Loneliness and isolation bring a tear
I'll help you with your cloud of fear

I was in Nam when a buddy I'd lose
Cost of freedom—you have to choose

Our flag's colors bright in the sun
These precious colors never run

The color of sacrifice shout and bellow
It is a rainbow without the yellow

I know "down" goes on for a long time
I prayed for a phone booth and a dime

Encouragement is like a vitamin from shelf
I thank you for doing and forgetting self

I love you guys—don't know your name
Good news—you're in my hero Hall of Fame

Landmines, snipers, booby traps too
I served in Nam and saw it through

I lived and came home by His grace
I am concerned—it shows on my face

I am partnering with you in this war
Each opportunity has a wide-open door

Thanks for all duty not seen on news
With your type, we win—not lose

Your service is way beyond measure
Contributions to freedom we treasure

May God's Word comfort you twenty-four-seven
Your name might be John, Jacob, or Kevin

Read this and know that I care—for sure
Partners in prayer, sun, wind to end

I think of freedom as the birds fly in
Thank you, friend, for taking it on chin

I think of freedom as grandchildren play
Heavenly father, protect them—I pray

Dynamics of freedom are on display
Protect me, friend—here in the USA

Nothing for granted—this vet, thanks
Thank God for everyone in the ranks

The sounds of freedom are all around
The blessings of freedom richly abound

This vet can flashback and see it all
Thanks for serving—you stand very tall

I can think forward too—to just wonder
Will posterity have to hear war's thunder?

Hear now the faint sound of beating drums
Posterity's heart beats as freedom hums

This message ends, and it is very, very clear
My country 'tis of thee—I hold soulfully dear

     ⌐   ⌐   ⌐   ⌐   ⌐   ⌐   ⌐   ⌐   ⌐   ⌐   ⌐

Written on occasion of praying for our troops in Iraq and Afghanistan. My grandchildren already know that Grandpa holds the flag in a deep part of his heart—and all those that have and are now serving. Others are giving dedicated service so I can continue to reap the benefits of freedom. Humbly, I say thank you, Lord, and may God bless, America.

     ⌐   ⌐   ⌐   ⌐   ⌐   ⌐   ⌐   ⌐   ⌐   ⌐

Flag Me Down

On this busy road of life
Stop me, please, amid strife

Help me see the worth of all
Show me flags standing tall

This veteran holds back tears
Freedom has won over years

Heritage so rich and deeply felt
Seeing flag makes sternness melt

Thanks, Lord, for those that died
May their souls with thee abide

Thanks, Lord, for colors that won't run
Price paid—now children can have fun

Thanks, Lord, when sun shines on flag
Beauty and meaning—about this I brag

Wave to me and show forth old glory
So proud to tell my grandkids the story

Wave to me and make my heart sing
Pray safely our troops home—you'll bring

Beneficiaries of sacrifice from long ago?
Flame of freedom, never lose your glow

May every American love freedom so much
They'll do their part to give freedom's touch

Old glory snugly hugs a fallen one's coffin
It's so very clear—he'll never be forgotten

The tombstones see the four seasons change
Do we show gratitude while home on range?

Loved ones file by in sun or in pouring rain
Hearts swell with pride—but still the pain

May freedom's flag wave shadows on grave
You gave it all—others freedom to save

We accept this gift—ole red, white, and blue
Lord, help us honor it—our whole life through

Across this land, people remember on July day
Color guard—in step—carries old glory our way

This republic has allegiance of our pledge
May we always vote to keep our living edge

What were the words of the fallen spoken?
A cry to family and country—love not broken

We know of noble and right—may we never sag
Undivided and under God—we cherish our flag

Flag us down, Lord, humble us in your way
Close to principles of greatness—we stay

We believe the USA is more than appointed
Our soul says it is really, divinely anointed

Respect flag—children need to know how
Thankful someday as hands steady the plow

Proudly
Our flag—my flag—these tears seem right

The enemy is out there—spewing much sin
Lord, help us that we crumble not from within

Thanks ole glory—symbol of hope—for bastion
Loving God and country—always in fashion

～　～　～　～　～　～　～　～　～　～　～

Written on occasion of seeing a beautiful flagpole and flag installed at Jordon and Karen's home. The flag makes me happy and sad at the same time. Happy for the rich blessings of freedom I have, and sad for the families who have lost loved ones. When I get to heaven, I want to greet all those that lost their lives, and as they did, they expected us to carry on with all that this awesome country stands for. There is also the Christian flag that reminds us of our Savior who died for our sins. He also is the only hope in the world for a purpose-driven life that continues on into eternal life. Amen and amen.

～　～　～　～　～　～　～　～　～　～　～

Enter Under Flag

We came to Virginia through the air
In a hurry with no time to spare

Son's family was a count of four
We're so happy to see their door

Everything was beautiful even trim
Our hearts were full to the brim

On the porch fixed with first class
Old glory waved above green grass

Our son's patriotism warms the soul
Children-loving USA is a special goal

A special scene locked in our minds
This love of country our hearts binds

Thanks, son, for this special treasure
I look at your home with such pleasure

⌐ ⌐ ⌐ ⌐ ⌐ ⌐ ⌐ ⌐ ⌐ ⌐ ⌐

Written on occasion of seeing Jon and Kori's home in Virginia during
October. The flag really was a beautiful finishing touch to a fresh paint job.
I remember walking with Logan when he was around two and stopping and
pointing out the flag. Sadly not enough people fly old glory. As for me and
my household, we will fly the flag of the best country in the world. May
something I do in my life make it a better place than when I arrived.

⌐ ⌐ ⌐ ⌐ ⌐ ⌐ ⌐ ⌐ ⌐ ⌐ ⌐

Are You Weeping, My Precious Flag?

The morning sunlight warmed slowly
My flag hung down as if lowly

Frost held fast the stars and stripes
Hold fast to the warrior that fights

A drip of water drops from the tip
Our symbol of unity—yes, bite the lip

More drops spaced and rhythmic fall
Flag is weeping for those on the wall

The flag is dry now, thanks to the sun
Stillness changed, movements begun

Old glory held high above the ground
The echoes of victory will resound

Gather children and listen so clear
Many have died to keep freedom near

Old glory has defended those oppressed
Were those enemies demon possessed?

Breathe deeply the air of liberty, lil' pal
Tears are still shed for those who fall

Go ahead and weep my precious flag
Your colors never run nor show sag

Tears of sorrow and joy now seem mute
Emotions rise and eyes glisten during salute

I pledge allegiance under God to thee
Old glory—divinely given from God to me

Written on occasion of seeing Jordan Russell's flag drying from a frost the night before. The sun and warmth caused a dynamic scene as moisture dripped from the lower tip of the flag. This caused me to reflect on how dearly I love my flag and this country. I want to see old glory always fly and wave the joy of hope for all to see . . . and for our children to know the price that was paid for their liberty. Thank you, Lord.

Powerful Wreath

The setting sun ushered the cool
Learning from reality's school

The wreath leans now on cross
Love grows but not old moss

This one paid the highest price
Thanks—my life is more than nice

Your life soon ended early on
A place in hearts—you've won

The finality of this scene is held
May Jesus hold you as you meld

Safe from danger and of pain
Jesus gives you joy and all gain

Cool breezes blow now over hill
You gave it all—we enjoy life still

Freedom costs, how much? Do tell
Here shows us the toll of that bell

Fed now by hearts of gratitude
Stray not far from this powered mood

The white cross reaches to God and us
Serve God and country add such a plus

Tears fall here—before, now, and after
Say thanks to God—look way beyond rafter

The wreath hugs the cross—oh evergreen
This act of love takes starkness from scene

Depart now as darkness blankets this fact
Lord, forgive us now for devotion lacked

Praise God, we are not at the end of our rope
We can see them again—Jesus gave us hope

Hold each other tightly as through this clime
Benefits of freedom help us sleep and dine

Thank you, wreath, for reminding me again
Here lies the remains of women and men

They speak volumes without saying a word
Thanks, God, I was here today, and I heard

Written on occasion of reading a true story of a man who donates thousands of wreaths to Arlington cemetery every year. Many others are getting involved, and it is heartwarming to see this outpouring of love for those who gave it all and for this God-ordained country. This is a tribute to my Vietnam buddies both under a white cross and the ones living. This is also a tribute to my Father Douglas Conrad Nordstrom who served in the United States Army during WW II. I also give tribute to my brother who served in the United States Army and to my late brother who served four years in the United States Marines and a tribute to my honorable son who served in the United States Marines and is currently serving in the medical field saving lives as a paramedic and field-training officer.

Will You Be There?

No more rice paddies and mines
My thought of home daily climbs

Will you be there to greet me?
Or will life's routines busy be?

I have seen life and death up close
Mosquitoes and heat a daily dose

Will you be there with a happy sound?
I've seen friend's blood soak the ground

We were friends, but you moved on
Things have changed—much is gone

I hope you are there to say "hi"
Part of me will always be wet eye

PTSD is short for stress always
Things trigger thoughts of fearful days

Will you be there with eagerness?
I seem to have grown years—I confess

Will you be there, or will you forget?
I've waited a year by you to sit

Help me touch home—it's been forever
Please help me from Vietnam to sever

When plane lands, and I get out
Will you be there to hear me shout?

I'll look up to heaven and cry
My country and freedom grip me, that's why

Will you be there when I look at VN wall?
I'll be bent in prayer—then I'll stand tall

Thank you, Lord, for bringing me home
Will you be there when praise I moan?

Can I tell you I can't sleep at night?
Flashbacks make me sweat with fright

I'm much older now and changed too
Will you be there and help me through?

＾　＾　＾　＾　＾　＾　＾　＾　＾　＾　＾

Written on occasion of remembering that no one greeted us at the airport nor did any of my friends from before show much joy in seeing me. My family loved me, and I think were just as stunned as me that I lived through that armored combat.

I called home from San Francisco, and Dad answered. I can still hear him crying on the phone—with lists of the fallen daily printed in the paper. It was tough on the whole family.

I was blessed by God, and now I am living out the debt of love I owe to my God, my country, and my loved ones. We now have eleven total with the five grandchildren. I love that song that says, "Strength for today and bright hope for tomorrow." God bless you. Amen.

＾　＾　＾　＾　＾　＾　＾　＾　＾　＾　＾

Rat of the River

Can anyone hear me the rat?
On a small boat in VN I sat

Left my wife of 1.5 years and babe
Babe was three months old—I fade

Thirty days of training in clutch
Can you hear my love and much?

Vietnam was my next big stop
Would I be shot dead and drop?

I was a kid in uniform and boots
Sent to stop terrorist gooks

Three friends and I were gunned
Boat was sinking, and I was stunned

Come over here is what I said
No response—they were dead

I survived that hell of a place
At home, I was spit in the face

My wife met me at airport lounge
She made me feel like a scrounge

She said I left you when off to Nam
This dagger to my heart, she did ram

Did she know, and did she care?
I served faithfully way over there

Patrolling the rivers—determined speed
We were sitting ducks—often in the lead

River rat, river rat, where did you go?

Partly out of my mind—fear did grow

Did you bother to write me—this wet rat?
I don't care at all about a Vietnam hat

My true stories bore you, it is clear
I'll shut up and hold them near

Don't talk to me with professional flair
You don't understand—you weren't there

Come to my shop—quietly I will cry
I lost more than you know-that's why

What I lost I'll never see again for sure
With God's help and VN brothers I'll endure

Anything you say just sounds very lame
Saw blood-guts and pain-you weren't in the game

My loss and pain fit me like a ball in the glove
Don't give me answers and down throat to shove

Besides God there is only one I can trust
He was there in the jungle and the rust

He knows the pains that won't go away
He prays for me each and every day

We share the deep soul felt pain
We endured the warm monsoon rain

Thanks for trying, but to you, I can't talk
I've tried to, but my words stop and balk

Leave—go back to place that you're from
Don't be upset—I'm waiting a call from Tom

Written on occasion of thinking about my buddy and true brother named Ken, who was a river rat for the navy in Vietnam. He and I both fight the battle of the emotional and mental scars from that place, but we understand each other and can talk about it. It is my privilege and honor to know this American war hero named Ken, and I salute him for his love of family and country. With a friend like Ken, you don't need to look for any more. Love ya, man.

Faith

Can't Sting Me

Media mountains avalanche down
Bad news spreads all over town

Freedom is such a sacrifice, my heart
Without devotion, I couldn't take part

I've received and taken for granted
"God bless, America," I've even chanted

Hating the Christians is the craze
Many think we are in the last days

Evil has become right in their mind
I trust God for all the daily grind

Rich and pampered and wanting not
Spiritual strength—have not sought

Fact, God is the blessed controller
From older to younger in stroller

We must love him with body, soul, mind
Otherwise, we are spiritually blind

Try and sting me, sin, it won't work
Jesus is in me, even though you lurk

I'm not in competition to get trinkets
Houses, cars, money, power, etc.

Praise God, my soul looks up to thee
Thou precious lamb of Calvary

The joy I have the world didn't give
Without it now, I just couldn't live

Oh Lord, many of your people are asleep
Their plan leaves out your love to keep

They have been stung by Satan's darts
No more concern for spiritual smarts

When they are stung enough, they'll say
Lord, I needed you, and you went away

Salvation secure, he never went away
More important, you thought, I'll stray

His Word, his love, his correction—joy
Strengthen me for any of Satan's ploy

Who is a Christian in this world of sin?
Does action show you have him within?

Try to sting me, you old hairless coot
Full armor of God makes sting mute

Your power is great, but his is heavenly
Greater than you and gives victory

Try to sting my life and fill it with pain
I'll live for him—but to die is real gain

I love you, Lord, and to you, my arms raise
Obediently, I offer my sacrifice of praise

⌐ ⌐ ⌐ ⌐ ⌐ ⌐ ⌐ ⌐ ⌐ ⌐ ⌐

Written on occasion of putting my trust in the Lord for this a new day. I trust
him to meet all my needs, and I trust him to help me share the living truth
I have and am experiencing. Victory in Jesus—for each trial that comes no

matter how big or how small. May I live for you, Lord, and forgive me when I don't. The world definitely is in heavy problems with wars and rumors of war. Lord, I pray for a revival of your spirit to sweep across land and into the hearts of unbelievers. I give to you my country, my family, myself—and request your care and guidance. Thank you, Lord.

Heaven Is Not Like Going Home

Heaven is not like going home
Out of your house, you've grown

You never come back to your house
It's left to spiders and maybe a mouse

Sometimes your room left as was
Nothing touched, well, just cause

Phone not answered—tub dripping
Mailman, this box is just skipping

Roof leaks and ceiling falls in sink
Soon the house has a musty stink

Owner oft said this house not needed
Going away, yes, spiritual truth heeded

Heaven is not like coming home
For this old house, I'll never moan

How could you leave your peace?
It was only as good as my lease

Said good-bye while lease ended
My work here was fully rended

Heaven is not like coming home, sir
Words can't tell the peace and mirth

It's more than these repairs and paint
Eternal rewards, and you're called saint

No more I'll leave the light on for you
Jesus light and glory shines through

Heaven is different in all aspects
No need for cash or writing checks

Long for heaven but while here still
Thirst for righteousness and his will

Seeds of love I sowed each new day
"Welcome home, my child," Jesus will say

My soul is leaving, and I change—now
When I see him, I pose in a long bow

Heaven is not like coming home, I say
Heaven is eternally better in every way

⁓ ⁓ ⁓ ⁓ ⁓ ⁓ ⁓ ⁓ ⁓ ⁓ ⁓

Written on occasion of our little granddaughter telling me that heaven is not like coming home—you never come back to your house. I asked her what heaven was like, and she said it is like being at home where God and Jesus live. Wow! She overwhelmed me, and I said I would write a poem about what she said. Yes, it is so precious to be with our grandchildren and experience their life and plant seeds of love from us and about our Lord and Savior Jesus Christ. "Turn your eyes on Jesus, and the things of earth will grow strangely dim—in the light of his glory and grace." Taryl also said that Grandma and Grandpa and Mommie and Daddy and J.T. are also going to be in heaven—going to go and meet Grandma Tarel who never knew her namesake—little Taryl.

⁓ ⁓ ⁓ ⁓ ⁓ ⁓ ⁓ ⁓ ⁓ ⁓ ⁓

G—d of T—n—s

Good things happen, and I say thanks
Just then, I'm lifted into emotional ranks

Obedient to what you have called me
Moment by moment, that's what I see

My trust is strengthened as in past
Divine Word says your love will last

Your love will carry through each test
All you want for me is your very best

I have so much now and heavenly blessed
Lots to do but too blessed to be stressed

Interesting time of transition for sure
Your precious love makes me secure

I am studying the body, your creation
So many people on earth in every nation

Each step of success, I am overjoyed
For now pushing my squeamish lamboid

Glimmer and tear come from the eye
I see my wife and son and take a sigh

Okay now under your blessed control
Green light forward, I'm on a roll

Lord, you've done much, and I say yahoo
Now I ask, what can I do for you?

⌐ ⌐ ⌐ ⌐ ⌐ ⌐ ⌐ ⌐ ⌐ ⌐

Written on occasion of serving a God of thanks. For Jonathan during that time leading up to his paramedic test.

⌐ ⌐ ⌐ ⌐ ⌐ ⌐ ⌐ ⌐ ⌐ ⌐

Help for the Leaning Challenged

What is it today? Worry or trust?
One has hope, the other is rust

Things could look bad and sour
Trust helps for each and every hour

Your companion could be ripe hope
Nothing about worry helps you cope

What is it that matters to you most?
Those things, does it help to boast?

God is the giver and definer of all
Trust helps you hold head up tall

Don't lean to the side of worry
It causes your future to look blurry

Whatever happens, trust goes first
Worry then, a former outburst

Trust calms body, soul, and spirit
Worry only causes you to fear it

Lean on good, trust, and just obey
Live with confidence—this, I will say

Dressed in God's full armor—for fight
Enemy my footstool—what a sight

Trust confidently—victory is the prize
See the world through Jesus's eyes

Take worry and put it in its place
Trust and trust—worry can be erased

Lean and trust—exercise faith every day
Lean on him while knees position to pray

Smile at the storm that life gives you
Joyous will be your color—not blue

Worry makes you play the blame game
Trust helps the problems look tame

Salvation and the creator's on call worth
Ask him for—he has loved you since birth

With trust, your way won't show swerve
You'll tell others—him you want to serve

Lean on him and let worry really be gone
Trust and pray, and you'll have a new song

Lean on trust—he'll never let you down
He'll forgive you when you act the clown

Trust and lean—victory is on a steady roll
Then say, "It is truly well with my soul"

~   ~   ~   ~   ~   ~   ~   ~   ~   ~   ~

Written on occasion of shaking off worry and trusting more for everything
that I need. It sure makes life more bearable and helps focus on things that
are more important and life changing. And God can use me to help change
someone else's life from the imprisonment of worrying. It has been said that
worrying is like a rocking chair. It gives you something to do, but doesn't get
you anywhere. Now lean so far forward you fall on your knees and cry out
to God for more of him in your life. God bless you. Here is the score:

trusting warrior = total victory
Worry wart = zero

~   ~   ~   ~   ~   ~   ~   ~   ~   ~   ~

The Unlocked Door

We anticipated the visit
No one would miss it

Winding up the stone path
The vines climbed up the lath

It is true—this door never locked
No stranger has ever shocked

Residents are known here and wide
Confidence in Jesus they do abide

Eat the fish, rice, and dash of soy
Lord's strength gives them joy

Nothing new nor fancy but clean
Fireplace mantle has good sheen

Relax and listen to words of truth
Hear stories like the love of Ruth

We have our Bibles a ring and a reel
Choose to rob us—no big deal

Door has no lock freely come in
Do you want the Savior to win?

We are never at the end of our rope
Jesus, our Savior, gives us true hope

Simple living—we have few clothes
We have valuable friends and no foes

We enjoy sharing about our Lord
His Word cuts like a two-edged sword

If you must leave, hurry back
With our Lord, see we have no lack

Written on occasion of talking with my best friend Don Smith. Prayer and encouragement are medicinal, and Don needed both. God bless, Don and Jewell. From Thomas, the lesser.

Delight

I stand at the window and see
The new day God has for me

This earth is thoroughly adorned
Many are seeking, some have mourned

Things around me make me a king
Some suffer without anything

I delight in you, Lord, my source
Our bond allows for no remorse

When all is bleak and no light around
I seek your face—knees on ground

Fears and doubts are put away
God's spirit shows a servants sway

I delight in this treasure—thanks, Lord
It can't be stolen—I have your word

These things grow dim under his light
Glory and grace take dark out of night

I delight in you Lord, let me serve
Uncomfortable zones touch a nerve

Let me see and let me do
Things with eternal value

You're my reliance, my friend
You can cause things to mend

I love you, Lord, with all my heart
Never leave me nor ever depart

Let me serve with heart so pure
Your spirit seen in me for sure

Not much matters in this worldly mess
Salvation power and true holiness

Encouragement hope and specialness
I want more of you, Lord, nothing less

Things will hurt and leave a real sting
I delight in you, Lord, love has a ring

Constantly abiding—Jesus is mine
Constantly abiding—glory divine

Special and precious, you say we are
Satan threatens to take us down in tar

Sacred delight fills my mind and heart
Nothing can separate us not even a dart

My gift to my loved ones, I cherish dear
To delight in you and to keep you ever near

Only one life it will soon be past
Only what's done for Christ will last

I delight in you—no longer a lost sinner
Changed forever, and now I'm a winner

ᕇ   ᕇ   ᕇ   ᕇ   ᕇ   ᕇ   ᕇ   ᕇ   ᕇ   ᕇ   ᕇ

Written on occasion of thinking about the character of God and evaluating my own areas of delight and areas of shortcomings. I want to be known as someone that people say delights in his Lord and Savior. I want to be a channel of blessing to those around me so that their spiritual needs will be met. Thank you, Lord, for choosing me to delight in you. Help me to become more like you.

ᕇ   ᕇ   ᕇ   ᕇ   ᕇ   ᕇ   ᕇ   ᕇ   ᕇ   ᕇ   ᕇ

Jumping Prayers

Karen and Jordan, I know you like prayer
Prayer can be single or layer upon layer

A jumping prayer causes something of a kind
With this, you know more of God's mind

Peace be still and know that I am God
Anything that occurs, we give him the nod

This prayer for peace jumps high and wide
Passes human understanding to him abide

This prayer clears the chasm of fear
This prayer allows him to hold us near

The question, why is not easy to answer dear
His blessed control is evident, it's clear

This prayer launches from the pad of sad
It lands on the site where a sign reads Glad

Our faith helps us in times of questions serious
How he'll see you through is so curious

His Word is not just feelings but solid fact
His blessings are so full and just so compact

With this prayer, we jump from dread to consolation
Moment by moment, we are kept in jubilation

When we land on joy, we know he is our prize
Our understanding goes beyond human eyes

Lord, right now I throw everything at your feet
I remember that to trust in you is so sweet

Thanks for the jumping prayers that give me calm
You are the great physician and so give me balm

I may need to pray again and jump to your side
This life, you have given me is such a big ride

I ponder and predict as I'm quiet as a mouse
I also know Jesus is the head of this house

～　～　～　～　～　～　～　～　～　～　～

Written on occasion of my dear Karen needing a word of encouragement
about her developing baby. Lord, this is my prayer for her that each moment
will be a soft landing in your hands after leaping and clearing the chasm
of human understanding. Lord, help Karen and Jordan and Taryl to know
the depth of my love. Help them to know that Bobbi and I stand ready to
assist in any and all ways needed. Blessed be your name on high. Moment
by moment, we trust in your amazing grace. From Grandpa Tom in honor
of my little pal Jackson Thomas Russell.

～　～　～　～　～　～　～　～　～　～　～

Emo Shuns

Lord, you know this house is grand
It served us well and was planned

Every square inch shows your love
Still fits just like a glove

Now we are leaving some each day
Soon we'll let Somerset sway

Gratefulness fills our hearts and minds
Somerset calls and just between the lines

We searched for the right place to arrive
Now we're settled and for now no more to strive

Emo Shuns for the old and joy for the new
Size and square footage and just the right hue?

God's will and just in time
Soon Somerset is where we'll dine

Emotions for this home really grew
Now I'll plant my heart in Somerset new

Changing isn't easy, Lord, there's a little sting
You'll help me, Lord, you are everything

Sweet peace will overcome me at the door
We'll now live here including no. 4

Lord, you have blessed us more than a ton
Now, Lord, I give you all my Emo Shun

This Somerset place to you, I dedicate
All who enter will appreciate

Above all your glory to shine here
Head of the house is Jesus so dear

May all who enter know of your love
For yes, it's true, this fits like a glove

My prince drives up now it is clear
Can't call him king 'cause he is already here

The children run to Daddy and jump up
Mother calls to the table to sup

Stories of the day and praise the Lords
This is now a home, yes, these nails and boards

Emo Shuns are here that walls can't contain
It is so beautiful here even in the rain

We are so blessed, it touches that nerve
The one that causes us to want to serve

Peace to all who here see your grace
The family of four now enjoys the fireplace

Help me, Lord, as I pray in this humble position
Guide my Emo Shuns during this happy transition

～ ～ ～ ～ ～ ～ ～ ～ ～ ～ ～

Written on occasion of thinking about all the blessings of the Lord. For Karen and Jordan and Taryl and baby from old Dad.

～ ～ ～ ～ ～ ～ ～ ～ ～ ～ ～

It Is Not Me, Lord

I pray, Lord, help me prepare
I read your Word and then I stare

I'm tired, worn, and holding on
Fill me with your strength and song

I know by habit who comes here
Guests please today and Satan jeer

My way would be to resign and be free
Jonah tried it and received a whale's degree

I know you've called me and such
Right now, I need your powerful touch

This spiritual clinic, I lead every week
It is not me, Lord, that seekers seek

Your Holy Spirit carries the burden
It is not me, Lord, that does the herd in

I make my life sometimes a mess
It is not me, Lord, it's your faithfulness

I look from the pulpit and just out there
Sometimes people doze, and some stare

When I am my weakest, then you are strong
Give me the strength to carry on

It is not me, Lord, 'cause I wouldn't bother
Let me see through your eyes and see other

Others, Lord, it is not just me
Forgive me, Lord, and others to see

Lift me up above the circumstances now
Empty of self, I before you bow

Refresh me again, Lord, and tell me anew
It is not me, Lord, seeking you I grew

If I am leading today, let me lead to you
People often let me down, put me in stew

Don't know why others only serve by a start
Touch them today, Lord, deep in their heart

It is not my brother or sister but me, oh Lord
That needs to hourly heed your Word

Confident and secure in my eternal crown and place
Joint heir with Jesus, and I'll know him face to face

It is not me, Lord, that can grow this church
Help me, Lord, to lead others to wholly search

It is not me, Lord, with greatness to cast
Make me a servant with the least and last

Humble me now, Lord, and make your Word
Cut me deep with the two-edged sword

Never let me forget your Son you sent
To be successful, make me transparent

All the help from seminaries near
Won't help until I am your man sincere

∽   ∽   ∽   ∽   ∽   ∽   ∽   ∽   ∽   ∽   ∽

Written on occasion of realizing the pastor is the shepherd of the flock but
Christ is the shepherd of all the flocks. And He is the One who is in charge.

∽   ∽   ∽   ∽   ∽   ∽   ∽   ∽   ∽   ∽   ∽

Are We There Yet?

Sometimes, Lord, I wonder
Why the road is always going up?

Will I blunder?
Or with thee to sup?

I see the last straw
Lying close ahead

This sticks in my craw
My heart feels like lead

Cheer is my need
Joy my only greed

Don't take me out
That would be the ease

I'll just shout, shout
Strength for now, please

~ ~ ~ ~ ~ ~ ~ ~ ~ ~ ~

Written on occasion of thinking about the tough trails of life we have to climb and how we must rely on God's strength and guidance.

~ ~ ~ ~ ~ ~ ~ ~ ~ ~ ~

Lessons

Girl of Prettiness

Cold day before Thanksgiving break
Girl enters high school, sees Jake

Jake sees her, and they say hello
She thinks he is a very nice fellow

One class together just before lunch
Their friendship was budding—a hunch

She fell in the rain, books scattered
Others just laughed, feelings tattered

Jake was near and helped her stand
Rain soaked, she was feeling bland

Jake, you were the only one that cared
They laugh at me too, this he shared

He helped her limp to the overhang
I don't care about that type of gang

His jacket felt warm as she shivered
Rain was heavy as it ran so rivered

Their eyes met, and they told so much
Girl of prettiness had a light touch

They were seniors and had life to gain
Girl of prettiness, so glad you came

His inner strength was evident to her
The falling event was now at a blur

I get out early, am free right now
I'll get you home, you'll see how

Office checked her out, his truck came
Girl of prettiness sat as a proud dame

His truck was noisy and bumpy and fun
Girl of prettiness rode as heater did run

Pulled up to her house—in rain did run
Met Dad at door and heard, "Thanks, son"

Girl of prettiness said, "Thanks, Jake friend
Jake decided he wanted more time to spend

Girl of prettiness stayed on his young mind
Girl of prettiness, wonder if I am your kind

Jake is special, don't care what people say
He helped me, others laughed on their way

Oh, Daddy, I think I love this guy—Jake is cool
Girl of prettiness, I really like my new school

Next day of school, a note came her way
Jake said, "Let's talk, okay"

These new friends soon even held hands
One Friday night, a kiss on her lips lands

Many kisses later, their hearts pound strong
Girl of prettiness, relationship not wrong

Graduation and working and college now
Time of parting brought furrows in brow

Jake drove to college in faithful old truck
Girl of prettiness had him in her heart stuck

A lot of things happened while parted away
Girl of prettiness longed with Jake to stay

From the beginning, their love was so deep
Girl of prettiness, I want only you to keep

Jake at twenty-two needed some peace in his single life
He really wanted girl of prettiness for a wife

He called her and said he was coming to town
Girl of prettiness knew Jake was no clown

They met at the gate, and a long kiss ensued
Their love boiled over, thoroughly brewed

Oh Jake, without you, I've had much strife
I've missed you so very deeply in my life

On bended knee, Jake the question did ask
I put my heart out there, not under a mask

Girl of prettiness breathed deeply and said,
Oh yes, Jake, and I'm so happy—heart is fed

Wedding was glorious, and all had great joy
Jake was so proud and handsome—she coy

They knelt and prayed for God's blessing full
Their life together would never be dull

To Christ and each other, they promised true
From the beginning, their love bonded like glue

～　～　～　～　～　～　～　～　～　～　～

Written on occasion of thinking about a hypothetical couple that didn't
let the crowd dictate to them how to act. They went on even though they
were laughed at. The Christian love in their family was wonderful as they
met each challenge that appeared. Girl of prettiness had two miscarriages
and then gave birth to their son and later to a girl of prettiness—daughter.

They all worked hard and played hard. Jake inherited the family farm, and the children loved their childhood. We leave this scene with Jake and girl of prettiness telling their children how they met—for the umpteenth time. The old pickup still ran and was sitting outside, loaded with firewood. It was a cold day before Thanksgiving break.

Help and God Bless

My car stopped at the red light
The person—cardboard—a sight

Seems they are everywhere to beg
What's her name? Maybe it is Meg

I give and work and share my life
Is guilt supposed to hit like a knife

Sometimes they look, face a smudge
I try so hard to not act like the judge

I don't know if they are really in need
Or do they want free money—a greed?

It troubles me most when a child sits
When the parent gets money in bits

People do give, and God bless them
Am I the rat for driving by—they a gem?

Mixed feelings keep entering my mind
I enter my world of the daily grind

It all adds up—here's a nickel or dime
Some wear shoes—much newer than mine

City services available—just sign up
No one has to use a sign and a tin cup

His sign said will work, he didn't take
Said he'd make more there, money rake

Once a double amputee sat in mobile chair
Gave him five dollars, I really did care

I like it when the light is green, I zip by
Don't have to sit there and catch an eye

I work for my money—in God do I trust
Is life this bad—to have this kind of thrust?

I sometimes give scripture or fresh food
They show no smile—yes, money was mood

Where do they live, and where do they go?
How much do they make, at this silent show?

So many cars, and so many see the sign
Would they go if you asked them to dine?

No more beggars—I'm far from their post
Wife calls cell phone, cooking a roast

Hugs and greetings—kisses at the door
How was your day dear—just a chore?

I'm grateful for what I have and more
Passing them up—something hits my core

Tell your story, tell the truth and all
I can't check it out, it is God's call

I just want to drive, get to my place
I don't like cardboard signs in my face

Tomorrow is another day, some ordeal
Give joy, you know what is fake or real

Promise not to get upset—for all day
They'll never know I drive by and pray

Written on occasion of getting upset that there are so many beggars, and they don't have to be. If I give to them, am I feeding a bad habit? It's not up to me. I'll continue to pray for them in this land of plenty. Can I ask for one more thing, Lord, a heart of gratitude?

That'll Be $2.49, Please

The small sign hung on the wall
Blessed sign and message so tall

Don't let too much of yesterday
Use up too much of today, I say

So many are plagued with guilt
Yesterday's stories make one wilt

Today is the day that God has made
In his Word, the foundation is laid

Children who knew abuse by others
For them, yesterday gives smothers

Anger made someone hurt for life
Memories cut the soul like a knife

Now the neglects can't be undone
Instead of love, the person does shun

$2.49 for this awesome little sign
Tall message on it fits anytime

If yesterday uses up much of today
Accept Jesus's plan and sincerely pray

Don't wait to say, "I'm really sorry"
I know now I lived the wrong story

I was a mean, cold-hearted jerk
You said you loved me—with perk

I missed your birthday for three years
Now I'm sorry, and I have big tears

Yesterdays were lost; can't go back
I reach out to you—with no love lack

How did you turn out to be a dear?
After growing up with such fear

Things are different now, my child
Jesus saved me, no longer am wild

Sure, let yesterday swallow me
Unlock your heart's door with key

Wow, you are married, son on way
Don't let yesterday keep us astray

Today is a new day, I sing in a choir
Yesterday hurts and is loaded mire

Yesterday is heavy torment in brain
To forgive me will be a huge strain

I always put you down, and you cried
Believe me, please, my eyes open wide

I called you bad names—shame came
I'm the only one guilty in blame game

Don't deserve your love, please try
Want to be in your heart—before I die

I loathe my past, but I must leave room
Some space for today—shut out gloom

$2.49 isn't a lot of value and money
What it says has helped me, honey

When you read this, please really know
I'm sober and clean and want to love you so

       ⌐   ⌐   ⌐   ⌐   ⌐   ⌐   ⌐   ⌐   ⌐   ⌐   ⌐

Written on occasion of meeting someone who hated their dad for destroying their childhood and causing lifetime scars. I prayed with them that they would leave a sliver of space for today and not let yesterday use up everything. Things changed for the better over time, and a little grandson learned the sincere love of his grandpa. By God's grace—the time remaining in the Grandpa's life was spent helping his daughter and grandson and, yes, the son-in-law. We leave them now at a big celebration. Grandpa found Grandma after years of separation, and they remarried in a backyard setting, overlooking a three-acre pond. The family was together again after all these years . . . with wisdom, power, and love. Our God reigns.

       ⌐   ⌐   ⌐   ⌐   ⌐   ⌐   ⌐   ⌐   ⌐   ⌐   ⌐

Day Off

Woke at five with head a spin
Now relax, no need to go in

This is Friday and ache in head
No work for three days instead

Love my job—people are great
A slow breakfast I just ate

Kick back and don't answer phone
Bask in the condition of "alone"

Clutter can happen—laundry—oh well
Put your feet up—now that's swell

This is the day to heal—use slow pace
Hot cup of tea and book—yes, fireplace

Read the Word—pray and hum and sing
Soon in your heart, joy bells will ring

Written on occasion of thinking about someone who might need a day off to get healed up. We need that once in a while, and extra sleep is valuable beyond measure. Sorry, I can't get to phone. Leave a message, and I'll call you back as soon as possible . . . zzzzzzzzzzzzzzzzzzzzzzzzzzzzzzzzzz.

To Observe or Participate

The big game was on TV
Such fun—the guys and me

Wife and son at home playing
Goodies on the tray lying

Ran out the door—son was busy
My pace would make anyone dizzy

Cell phoned, my son said, "I'll be back"
His voice was sad—there was a lack

Thought about it long and hard
Son is alone—could play in yard

Turned around and hurried home
Son was humming—sounded like a poem

I picked him up and hugged him so
Seemed just then I saw him grow

He asked why I came back now
I said I missed you—why and how

You are five and can catch the ball
Run out long, and I'll give the call

This is fun, Dad, but not the big game
I wanted to be with you, more to gain

Life has moments to share and give
Being together helps me really live

Son fumbled the ball and chased it down
Dad didn't fumble and act the clown

Written on occasion of a dad wanting to participate instead of simply observing a football game. We leave this scene with the dad answering his cell phone and explaining why he didn't show up. Just then the son kicked the ball that the dad was holding for him, and they both cheered. Honey, our son is beyond thrilled with the backyard time. He keeps talking about it.

Impalming

The mortician said, "May I impalm you?"
Can't you wait man, get a clue

I still love life and want lots more
Impalm me, and it's the end of the score

Please let me impalm you—feels good
Impalm me, and I'll feel just like wood

Resist impalming, and I'll feel real sad
Don't impalm me, and I'll feel real glad

Impalming doesn't take long—just believe
After you are impalmed, you'll be relieved

I'm out of here—want nothing of it
Don't need impalming—I feel very fit

Special and precious—that's you friend
Impalming, you won't be the end

Stretch out your hand—greet once more
Give me your hand, this I implore

When I impalm you, I shake your hand
When I embalm you, you have left this land

⌐ ⌐ ⌐ ⌐ ⌐ ⌐ ⌐ ⌐ ⌐ ⌐ ⌐

Written on occasion of talking with my mortician friend and shaking his hand. The word *impalming* popped into my mind, and I don't even know if it is a word. If we ever meet, may I impalm you?

⌐ ⌐ ⌐ ⌐ ⌐ ⌐ ⌐ ⌐ ⌐ ⌐ ⌐

Look the Other Way

The bills were stacking up on desktop
My account is empty, oh, what a flop

I am a child of the king, he knows my need
He wants me to shed all forms of greed

I see a new pickup and boat down the lane
A foreclosure sign nearby shows real pain

My job was downsized, and so was I
Jesus only, Jesus only is my daily cry

I look the other way when temptation hits
I resist, and Satan just stomps and spits

There is an answer on the way, oh Lord
That answer is in your Word the sword

In two months, the house will be taken
My faith in you, Lord, will never be shaken

We've sold everything that we could, Lord
We will always walk with you in one accord

Debts aren't large, and tithe has first place
World's goods are dim in light of your grace

I looked the other way when a buyer came
I sold the ole pickup of Grandpa's—what a shame

I looked the other way as it moved away
Hugged my family and said, "God helped today"

God has never let us down—not even now
We need you, Lord, and before you, we bow

We went to church and sang of your love
Lord, what do we do? Answer starts above

I look the other way when my plans fail
I only look to you, Lord, as I set my sail

Today, guide my thoughts and actions, please
Make me the best steward of money and fees

Calm me, Lord, with thoughts of the sparrow
Provide as a bull's-eye is hit by arrow

Your timing is perfect, your strength is sure
You give the perfect ability to always endure

My pride is gone—I know I need some help
Knowing you are with me, I'll never yelp

With Jesus, there is victory—I'll not give up
I go to his table of grace and mercy to sup

You know, Lord, that I don't feel very bold
Praise you for strength—my children to hold

I wait on you, Lord, my mind is free of fright
Your joy is my strength—carry me tonight

Just when I need him, Jesus is there
Ever to comfort, ever to cheer

I don't know about tomorrow—I live today
I live through sunshine or clouds of gray

I look the other way when foundations sag
My foundation is you, Lord, and you never lag

Be still, my soul, the Lord is on your side
I leave life to you to order and provide

~   ~   ~   ~   ~   ~   ~   ~   ~   ~   ~

Written on occasion of thinking about the economic downturn and all the trouble people are having. Some are getting their greed meter checked and others are discovering what really matters in life. I believe we can live on less and with less. We leave this scene with the father leaving the house looking for work because he believes that God will provide. Along the way, he encourages others that haven't found the secret to successful living. Be weak enough to listen and strong enough to wait. This man just gave out a Bible, and his new friend is reading John 3:16.

~   ~   ~   ~   ~   ~   ~   ~   ~   ~   ~

My Check Arrived

This presidential wife has been paid
Students were given—foundation laid

No price can match what I've derived
Started happening day I arrived

Studying hard—no room left in head
Quitting is out—God called instead

I've taught, mentored, encouraged life
Helped students through tough strife

World's treasure would be so prudent
Couldn't pay for love from a student

My check has arrived in so many ways
Sometimes coming on time on blue days

Fancy receptions—so prim—I did my part
Who can price the sharing of your heart?

Sometimes I was being the Mrs. Dr. Phil
I would help wives marry to a pill

How many times was a scripture read?
Helped many when hope seemed dead

Returning the check—void on its face
Just too small—compared to his grace

President's wife, representative—oh yes
My smile was genuine, really, no less

My pay comes without clapping and roar
Touching lives is what I really adore

Leaders and followers stand in my line
Each one sincerely pursuing him—divine

My pay couldn't be gold and diamond rocks
I'm paid each time I read thank-you's in box

My pay couldn't come with full-piece band
My thread continues to a heavenly land

The doorbell sings—phone rings—and yes
People still need me—godly more not less

"Moment by moment, I'm kept in his love
Moment by moment, I've strength from above."

ﹾ ﹾ ﹾ ﹾ ﹾ ﹾ ﹾ ﹾ ﹾ ﹾ ﹾ

Written on occasion of thinking about college days and how leaders
influenced my life. Dr. Patterson must be special because my sis Connie
Johnson wouldn't say so if it wasn't true. God bless you and thank you
for your service both past and present. Yesterday is ashes, tomorrow is
firewood, only now the fire burns brightly. From Connie Johnson's brother
Tom Nordstrom—Vietnam combat infantry survivor and prostrate cancer
survivor. I've been paid also, and there was so much pay I need to share it
with others.

ﹾ ﹾ ﹾ ﹾ ﹾ ﹾ ﹾ ﹾ ﹾ ﹾ ﹾ

Rolf of Magnolia

Rolf was a dog who alerted the house
Somebody was coming—friend or louse

In the early days, he would run and jump
Now he enjoys lying around on rump

The magnolias would wave in the breeze
Every opportunity to alert he would seize

He wondered if his alert was doing good
None looked as he barked as he should

Soon he would only go half way to the gate
He was so tired of the food on his plate

He was tolerated now and felt unloved
Pet me, please, with your hands so gloved

I would bark up a storm, but who'd care?
Long time since a brush brushed my hair

I longed for the day little Logan'd visit
He would throw me a ball—not to miss it

Magnolia's called for Rolf and Logan
Two pals together is our own slogan

We walked, and he talked in English to me
I spoke dog with a limited vocabulary

Fetch, treat, sit, run, stay, others and more
He said I was smart and showed me adore

We went everywhere—I would sniff out
Rolf what did you find with reliable snout?

We'd return home, and I'd sleep outside
Master and dog—tomorrow we'll abide

Logan's birthday came and pictures taken
Rolf was left out and was a little shaken

Logan whistled and Rolf jumped with joy
Times were so special with this young boy

Come to the party, Rolf—celebrate with me
I love you, Rolf—you're part of the family

Written on occasion of remembering my childhood dog/pal named Blackie.
I am thinking about how grandson Logan likes to check things out and do
adventurous quests. I am looking forward to having lunch in a backpack and
Logan and his dog Wyatt, and I go for an adventure. One more companion
will make it complete. Logan's daddy will come too, and that is so very neat.
Breathing fresh air and feeling the warm sun and feeling free so much to
do, and we don't need TV.

The Old Lane

What a view as I visit here
The changes are so clear

Over there is old Elmer's house
That debris must have a mouse

His house was always trim and clean
Elmer wouldn't want his house seen

Cracked streets and broken curbs
Old events now are history blurbs

Trees seemed so big when as a child
I would kick the leaves when piled

Country store is now boarded up
Under the overgrowth is a truck

I stop now at the place we lived in
Memories of some things brought grin

It was new first time we entered door
Condition now is looking very sore

Fort in tree was a blissful place
Time has accomplished an erase

A lot of things we grip and hold
Soon, however, they could show mold

What is worth finding joy in?
Things that are made of wood or tin?

We strive and get them and behold
Sooner than we want, they are old

What, therefore, keeps our focus true?
Is enough enough, or are we still blue?

Our hope does not lie in the payments
Our hope is never found in raiments

People gawk and say, "I wish I had that"
Things are as important as a doormat

Someone might say, "You are really rich"
So much debt though, and here is a ditch

Strip it all away and what is left
A person who has nothing but bereft

Treasures are in heaven, stored with heart
Pictures, cars, and trinkets we can depart

Things and resources are gifts from God
Seeking the praise of men is slip and shod

The things of earth will grow strangely dim
He will keep us from feeling out on limb

The praise of men is eventually cruel
Praises of men do pay you in full

There is no gain nor is there any peace
Lift your eyes above things now on lease

We'll pass from this life to realms of glory
Without Christ as Savior, it's a different story

Hope in eternal life won't get old or sorry
With this hope, there is peace and no worry

Born, died, and then arose from the grave
Those who accept Him—He will surely save

The old lane is something we can think about
The good news is something we can shout

Peace won't come and last with payments
No real joy in shopping for more raiments

After the wedding and debts pile very high
Some people run away and just say good-bye

Darkness falls on the lane as I ponder
From the old church comes— "called up yonder"

I turn away from this trip to my past
I continue my tight grip on him with last

A purpose-driven life is waiting for you now
Ask him to forgive your sins as you bow

Written on occasion of praising God for his spiritual blessings and factual hope for the future. The Elmer mentioned in poem is Elmer Perkins who lived in the first gas station north of the California border in Oregon. He was an old bridge builder and later used to carry bodies up to the cemetery on "boot hill." He had lost one hand and wore a hook on that arm. Loved to sit by his old woodstove and listen to the stories of yesteryear. The Jones's mentioned in poem—no longer put on the dog before their neighbors because they went bankrupt and now live in section eight housing with their six children. They broke down on the freeway one rainy dark night and then went to the Baptist preacher's church that helped them on the freeway. Their life is much happier, and they are working hard to get out and stay out of debt. Mr. Jones now honors his wife and has been known to bring her flowers for no special day. The children now respect their father and obediently sit in the pew making a total of seven. Each one shouts out a hearty good night, and soon, all the lights will be out.

Sad

She was going to be sixteen
Drugs and alcohol were between

Dropped out of school, ha-ha
An alcoholic that woman Ma

Ma and distant Pa got divorced
She had emotions that scorched

Most of her friends—from school
Moved on—she just wasn't cool

Invitations by mail and phone sent
No one came to her party—how bent

Reality set in hard as she felt lonely
Her beauty had now turned to homely

Party had been set but now a sight
No one was there the candles to light

Neighbor across street asked why cry
No one came to my party that's why

It's my fault—I'm a mess, I need a fix
Prostitute, druggy, dropout is my mix

Written on occasion of feeling sad for my neighbor who was living the wild
life but was still a child at heart.

Less Than a Thousand

The key was cold, and the building lacked heat
I believed today one of miracles, devil to beat

Less than a thousand would attend today
For more, I shall always pray

Precious Holy Spirit you are the soul changer
Jesus from the start, you spoke from the manger

I pray for each pew and the people there to sit
At the front now, I know God's love furnace will be lit

I review my sermon, and each verse means so much
Lord, I ask for one thing more, your empowering touch

Many losses and tests that are only a sign
That every day you are helping me walk your line

Take all my weakness and make me strong
Build in me a very wonderful new song

Your message goes out to many now in the dark
The Holy Spirit never misses the mark

Make me transparent that me they do not see
Sins were forgiven on that victorious tree

Your Word speaks clear as souls you build
Your Words most beautiful, needing no guild

The key is warm and so is your house
Forgiveness is powerful no more feeling like louse

They call me the pastor and the guide
Like King David, let me do your will and abide

Another sermon to prepare and present
Anything done is from you and is lent

Blessings and joy keep filling my life cart
Give me one thing more, Lord, a grateful heart

~   ~   ~   ~   ~   ~   ~   ~   ~   ~   ~

Written on occasion of praying for Rev. Don Smith and wife, Jewell, and their ministry in their church.

~   ~   ~   ~   ~   ~   ~   ~   ~   ~   ~

Leaf of Winter

Summer's warmth has stepped aside
Winter's leaf wants to happily abide

Only leaf up in this grand tree
Holds through storms aggressively

I wait for you here on the ground
I promise my foot will not pound

I'll pick you up as a cherished one
The leaf of winter, I'll say I've won

Didn't want you to fall—yet I did
Would you land on point or a slid?

I think about you and stubborn grip
When you fall, will you make a flip?

Must go, but wait till I get back
Just now, I shall put wood in a stack

You look grand as you royally wave
Last bastion of summer—shade gave

Out of place just one leaf—up and alone
Example of perseverance is shown

When you fall, will you land on my head?
A definite bull's-eye but not of red

Your colors blend from dark to light
All of you made such a grand sight

Stiff winds blow, and you don't give up
Are you the tree's guard—you say yup

Thanks for service so steady and true
You were there through dry or dew

You've won the prize—above the crowd
Mystery surrounds you like a shroud

Can I learn a lesson from you, leaf friend?
Sinners need heart condition to see mend

We hold to ourselves till we're last on stage
We think we can do everything—so we gauge

We can gently come down into the arms of Him
Freedom and security come, and sins get trim

Let go and let God and often sit very still
What could be better than being in His will

Rake aside all the other leaves—watch a debut
God through Jesus—transforms and makes new

I look at the whole scene and just stand in awe
You truly love me, and love is constant law

I leave this chill and to warmth make a retreat
From my window, I'll see thee—champion of feat

Not interesting if all leaves fell all at once
Suddenly, their beauty would be lying in bunch

These thoughts, I'll cherish—keep my word
These ponderings point me to the Lord

Lord, am I like the first leaf—just to let go?
Or am I like the last leaf—my grip to show?

Show me, Lord, I'll know when to hold 'em
Help me let go and trust—with some bolden

All the leaves must fall—but just when
God knows and shows—every day—often

Few will take note nor long remember
This leaf of winter—holding tro December

Rejoicing in spirit and body feels good
Good night, leaf friend, still high in wood

Written on occasion of thinking about turning over a new leaf and listening
to the rain outside. Many times I've been alone pondering the Lord while
walking and stopping to observe something. You will like knowing that the
young man picked up the leaf the next morning and pressed it in a heavy old
book. He finished pressing it and mounted it with this caption. Oh Lord,
let me know and do your will. I trust you to guide and guard me until I see
your face. Later in life, his granddaughter climbed up on his lap and asked
him to tell her about leaves—a very special time.

This Model Is an A

Childhood memories include the model A
A good ole car could even haul hay

First vehicle I drove with my great Pop
Cherish those times—didn't want to stop

A special car that was faithful to serve
The first time I drove, it took some nerve

That engine had that familiar updraft carb
One time, we hauled large bags of rhubarb

I liked it—two doors and running boards
We pulled a trailer with wood in cords

The cab was cozy with the muffler, the heater
I cherish it now—that good ole Ford two-seater

I loved that car, and maintenance was simple
Much room under hood—you could hide a dimple

Just love old *a*'s—in the day or in the dark
Floor shift, throttle handle, and retard spark

It was a comfortable world in that cab for two
Dreamed of driving a girlfriend out for stew

Those were precious times—Dad and I and the A
Close my eyes, and I'm there again—but not to stay

Learned to shift without looking—didn't ride clutch
Dad and the Ford were good to me—loved them much

I close my eyes, and we are going to the Shell
Gas was twenty cents, and they had lots to sell

Lift the hood and listen to the idle—ooga horn too
No smog check—catalytic not there—smoke not blue

Not to worry—only an oil change—Ford in ole shop
Going to go now, but my A memories will not stop

Written on occasion of thinking back on how much Dad loved me and allowed me to experience so many things. This poem is dedicated to my sweet Pop and the awesome old A.

There's another guy who thinks Fords are no. 1. Dave Deming, the demo man. Give him a coffee as he drives up in an A. He'd be happy and have something to say. "Please stop the film and roll it back to the fifties. Put me there with an A and a coffee, and I'd have a lot to say."

Tears at the Mission

If you want dinner, listen to preaching
It's never too late—just start reaching

Jesus is there with arms open wide
He's the one to help you cross divide

You once had a family—but they left
Your wife tried, but she was left bereft

Tomorrow your daughter is sixteen—no you
Fear caused them to be deeply blue

Worry for her—wonder what she'll do
They moved out of state—established new

Your son needs a dad—to teach him things
At thirteen, he really wants you and it stings

Wife divorced you when found you cheated
Here you are a broken man—in mission seated

Many are your losses—tonight make a gain
Put it all on the altar—call out Jesus's name

Your life was spared in the hospital that night
Doctors were losing hope—nothing was bright

God kept you alive—for you to do his will
Now that he's your Savior—he'll give thrill

His thrill to you will be you seeing his grace
Tears here in the mission—not hopeless case

AIDS virus and medication bottle has one pill
When you run out—will there be a refill?

You've accepted Jesus—he gives the only hope
Life has consequences—with him you can cope

Lets pray right now for the family you had
Protect and guide them—you are their dad

Tears in this mission—God has met your heart
He'll never forsake you—close from start

Enrolled in the mission program but so weak
I pray for his genuine and his seeking streak

Later in my car I drive to my castle with loves
My children greet me—they seem like doves

I feel drained and really sad for that guy
Wrong decisions and life can slip by

My wife and I chat—children play on floor
What a happy world coming in my door

I tell the kids of tears that fell tonight
We prayed for him—and turned out light

I said I loved you—to each one in turn
Lord, make me a dad to teach and learn

I remember what my daughter said to me
If I didn't have you, Dad, I'd be so empty

Tears in the mission—I see them tonight
Lord, in your power—make this life right

Help him turn to you and away from regret

~ ~ ~ ~ ~ ~ ~ ~ ~ ~ ~

Written on occasion of thinking about the deep regret a man shared at the altar after I spoke at the mission in Santa Rosa. Even now I pray that he was able to contact his family and let them know how much he is sorry and that he loves you Lord. That may not have been possible, but I know your love, Lord, overcomes bitter hatred and remorse—and hatred for someone that has abandoned you and let alcohol and drugs take over as the new love. I pray too that the day of her birthday that his daughter develop a desire to someday see her dad. That this would be her quest. Oh yes, I'm sure there would be tears at her mission.

The Old Key

It was a blustery day out there
I was froze to the bon, I declare

I walked to the door of the church
I started for the key to search

My pants were old but no holes
Where could the old key be—fowls?

Birds were pecking and hunting good
The rice from wedding were the food

No key in my pocket—what's going on?
I must get in—either pro or con

Furnace to be lighted and lamps adorned
No key—no entrance—sure to be scorned

Did I lose it—loan it—or place it somewhere?
An answer, please—even out of thin air

Gave it to God—and prayed for creative thought
My frozen toes paced me my emotions wrought

The only key is lost, and I wish I knew where
People will be coming, and boy, will they stare

The matches were ready—furnace will be cold
Whatever I do, it must be really bold

Tempted to put up notice—no church today
Please help me potter—I am the clay

He touched the matches—wanted to be warm
A new thought hit him—like an alarm

Get old leaves and wood and make a fire
A different service—with warmth to inspire

Much effort produced a nice, warm blaze
No one will freeze—hope everyone stays

Grandma Duncan came and sat in her surrey
Singing started, and snow stopped flurry

Mr. Macintosh prayed—everyone recited amen
Salvation is true and lasts—not for to lend

Pastor's message—prepared long before
Are you a Christian outside this door?

The message was well received—phew
Reach out, reach out, after sitting in pew

The world needs Jesus—go and tell
I'd rather have Jesus and heaven—than hell

Sun peaked—children in snow were clowney
Mrs. Hamlin came—everyone given a brownie

Mrs. Duncan said—message wasn't to be missed
Thank you pastor for you taking the risk

Through a window, a deacon entered in
Pastor walked through open door—no sin

Thanks deacon Bob—hands did a firm squeeze
Let's look for key—no need to burn leaves

Sitting at my desk, I remember using the key
Then all I remember is letting God hear a plea

I sit here again and wonder what I did
Maybe here I'll recall where key is hid

The message was on II Chronicles 7:14
This verse is packed—so very much to be seen

I opened to that verse and noticed a clue
I had written—this is pertinent and so true

I quickly stood up with surprise on my face
There was the lost key in that biblical place

God had a reason—of this, I am sure
That message pastor—in my memory will endure

No one can say—the truth I have not seen
The key is there in 11 Chronicles 7:14

~ ~ ~ ~ ~ ~ ~ ~ ~ ~ ~

Written on occasion of thinking about churches and old keys. I enjoy reading II Chronicles 7:14 over and over because it has the formula for successful Christian living and the answer to our nation's ills. Bless the Lord, oh my soul, and all that is within me bless his holy name. The key person read the key verse and took key action to minister in a key manner to someone who needed a key to unlock a seemingly impossible situation. Heal our land Lord! God bless and keep you friend. Excuse me, I have to find my keys.

~ ~ ~ ~ ~ ~ ~ ~ ~ ~ ~

Not Much Damage

Just three, I knocked over the vase
Fun crayoning the wall hard to erase

At four, the fit I threw was a grout
Dad said no bike and long time-out

Five—I fell in the paint—ruined the hutch
One hundred fifty—very old since I was five and such

Six was the time I stole a choc. drop
Mouthwatering appeal—and no prop

Seven, I acted up in church with warning
Life magazine in pants—only a scorning

Eight was the apple hitting the truck
Good arc good timing—windshield struck

Nine saw the theft, and I was so guilty
Had to bury it on somebody's realty

Ten was when I ruined a car battery
Looked forward to Dad—and clattery

Eleven dreamed of the girl uptown
Wish she thought of me more than a clown

Twelve, I drove something for an hour
Surprised Dad wasn't more than sour

Thirteen, I stole several jars of apricots
A tribute to Mom—I could eat lots and lots

Fourteen, I was leveling off on pranks
More mature now—higher in the ranks

Stole a kiss at the mature age of fifteen
I thought I was suave with brill cream

Not much damage at sixteen and peeling out
Gutless—barked—little asphalt snout

Lost my heart at seventeen as I left for school
Tackled the big city—tried to be coooool

Damaged the enemy in Vietnam scene
Fear could grip you—even in the spleen

Completely wrecked a girl's single life
Glad I did—she is an angel my wife

Worked a lot and never went on skids
My angel wife thought it better—two kids

Not much damage now—better foresight
Don Smith was correct—honey, you're right

Seems like yesterday—banged pots and lids
Now it is such a joy to entertain grandkids

Not much damage, but they sure disappear
Cookies go with kids and Grandpa near

Grandpa answers the whys, whens, and snap
Yawn with me as I explain why we daily nap

Not much damage now—fixing some honeydews
Jesus helps me as I sit and think of life's clues

　　　　　ﾉ　ﾉ　ﾉ　ﾉ　ﾉ　ﾉ　ﾉ　ﾉ　ﾉ　ﾉ　ﾉ

Written on occasion of contemplating the years of childhood and growing
pains.

　　　　　ﾉ　ﾉ　ﾉ　ﾉ　ﾉ　ﾉ　ﾉ　ﾉ　ﾉ　ﾉ　ﾉ

How Much Flood Do You Want?

Water is like life to me
Enough for now, you see

Rain can be pain or blessing
Can be the feathers or dressing

When rain is pain, we float
We say God has really smote

We really struggle with only one oar
We cry out to God, "Don't give me more"

Our little boat goes in circles now
Floodwaters are up to the brow

Circling boat goes downstream
Stress and pressure gather steam

Before we drop over the deadly falls
A still small voice calls

I obey and quickly receive help
Plucked from danger, I yelp

On shore and danger now behind
My life's film needs a rewind

When did I begin to paddle with one oar?
That's when I failed to trust and soar

Never too late to take the eagle ride
High above the circumstances to glide

Floods of pain used to be so wrong
Pains now blessings with a new song

Two oars and a course charted only right
Leaving His will now would be a blight

Sailing for Jesus through rough and clear
His comfort confidence and guidance near

Rain now turns me to living water deep
Floods of blessings, I cherish and keep

Lord, don't give me a bumpless ride
Strength for obstacles 'cause you're inside

Floods will swamp, and clouds block the sun
His strength is mine and victory's won

I dock now briefly with hull full of joy
I unload my cargo of encouragement croy

Line up on the dock, those with only one oar
Turn away from self and knock at his door

Grace through faith, there is no other anchor
Our status the same whether hand or banker

He throws out the lifeline so very delf
Someone might miss it while looking at self

Oh Lord, how much flood do I really want?
My line to you will always be taunt

First, flood me with blessings like rain
I can handle anything, even the pain

~ ~ ~ ~ ~ ~ ~ ~ ~ ~

Written on occasion of reflecting on spiritual lessons I've learned. Written for Jonathan, our wonderful son, and for Karen, our wonderful daughter.

~ ~ ~ ~ ~ ~ ~ ~ ~ ~

Sailfish

My boat is named *Sailfish*, 100 percent loved
Loaded and happy—from dock shoved

No wife, no kids, no pets—just all me
All for myself and not an added fee

Sailfish fits me, and I am really good
Sky darkens, and I pull up my hood

That is unusual—a shark swims close
Didn't bring charts—I trust myself

Whipped waves toss *Sailfish* around
No fear in me can ever be found

Decks get swamped, and engine stops
Another huge wave hovers and drops

Everything is wet, but I am the real deal
Bobbing and twisting—I lose my last meal

I try to start the engine with a tool
I check the tank, and I am out of fuel

Afternoon sky turns to night so fast
Another wave and slam—no more mast

Remain calm—this is just a serious test
My wisdom—my skill—I've always been best

Waves and bobbing and night is stark
Another waves hit, and I see a shark

Sailfish rolls and bobs, almost capsizes
I can do it—*Sailfish* is hammered but rises

Sailfish capsizes, and I cut my arm on rail
The shark comes closer, slapping its tail

Suddenly, I am lifted, and I see a bright light
Head throbbing, body spent—this isn't right

I know I was eaten—and to a dream did slip
Fact is, I was rescued by a passing ship

Sailfish is gone, and I don't really care
Please let me tell you thoughts I share

I was full of myself and going nowhere
I got to the point that for others I didn't care

I was dead in myself, no power to be real
Thought I could do anything—think don't feel

My *Sailfish* ways are gone and history
Blood and the shark—rescued—a mystery?

Once, I cried out, "God, please make this cease"
In your time, you did—and now I have peace

Peace, power, and purpose are mine now
No more *Sailfish* ways—to you, I humbly bow

The fear and the loss of that night—are blurred
Lord Jesus, I am changed—now I cherish your Word

~   ~   ~   ~   ~   ~   ~   ~   ~   ~   ~

Written on occasion of praising God for how lives are transformed. We leave this scene, and months later, we see this man is now married and is out in the garage making a small boat. They have just found out their first child will be a son. Honey, I am ready to name this boat for our son. Oh ya. Yes, and there will be nothing *Sailfish* about it. It will be called Rescued. The garage light is turned out, and behind the door, he asks, "Do you think he'll love me after I tell him how stupid and *Sailfish* I was?"

~   ~   ~   ~   ~   ~   ~   ~   ~   ~   ~

The Old Bike

The day it was new, I held it in awe
My eyes looked it over, it stuck in my craw

That bike was a companion each day
Hard to go in from such joyful play

Tires soon were dirty and full of grime
I felt such joy knowing it was mine

Freedom was nice as I rode in the wind
I would sometimes coast, my face grinned

My dog would run along dutifully
Tires made the bumps and no spree

Basket on front would carry from the store
When delivered home, I would ride more

Training wheels came off in short order
I would ride ever wider, seeking a new border

It grew smaller as I touched flat-footed
Cold days I ride with gloves and hooded

Another bike came along to meet my need
I can't forget my old bike, this I creed

Rust peeked through the paint and tires flat
Fast downhill off would fly my hat

Would ride my bike well or with a cough
Safety first or gravel spill was rough

Looking back memory, bells do ring
The old bike gave life for me a zing

I oft pondered the gears and chain
I was tough and oft rode in the rain

Once I confidently grew in my pace
I was tempted to ask someone to race

Bald tires and kick stand all askew
Paint now has a much lighter hue

Riding then I was tall and lang
When school was out, I rode and sang

Showing off for girls was futile and improper
They cared less and put me as a clodhopper

My bike was my steed as I rode into battle
My imaginary enemy had teeth to rattle

My old bike on a summer morn did arrive
Now I can go to memory pool with a dive

I didn't know it was coming what a surprize
It was beautiful and just my size

Thanks, Mom and Dad, with stun in my voice
How did you know this was just my choice?

Old bike disappeared in time, I don't know where
One can't keep everything and pile up in the air

First things carry memories that are not slanted
The surprise, joy, and freedom aren't for granted

Ride your bike not slow, or you will wobble
Pedal strong and safe and do not dawdle

The hill you are climbing, stressing lung and cord
When you coast down other side, it's your reward

I'd ride back into that scene again right now
I'd ride hard, and there is sweat on brow

When there, I would stop and look forward and back
Was I fuller then or is it now that I lack?

Snow is thick and falling just as I like
Times like this, I walk after parking my bike

Lessons to be learned from bikes as you grow
Life has low branches, keep your head low

Bikes come to ravines that are wide
Jump them or bridge them, you must decide

All bikes handy, and some are really cool
Ride with the companion wisdom, not fool

Come on, old bike, let's ride some more
Wheels of memories pedals of lore

~ ~ ~ ~ ~ ~ ~ ~ ~ ~ ~

Written on occasion of seeing one of Jonathan's childhood bikes. Karen also rode the trike. Keep on riding, don't ever stop. More riders coming—a new crop. Dedicated to the little pedal pushers named Taryl and Logan. Do your brakes work well?

~ ~ ~ ~ ~ ~ ~ ~ ~ ~ ~

Roberto, Ring That Bell

I heard the bell, and my throat was dry
He was pedaling the cart—do I buy?

Something about him—spirit of joy
Ring that bell and don't ever be coy

He really seemed to enjoy what he did
If he had problems, his smile they hid

Children eagerly bought ice cream
This was an honest job—but no dream

Pedaling the ice cream cart along—yes
He didn't make very much profit—I guess

Roberto, ring that bell—yes, you know how
The kids are running up so get ready now

Roberto, ring that bell—feel good yourself
You have what is priceless—your wealth

Your wealth not in money or things
Your inner happiness when the bell rings

I learned from you today—man of cheer
No matter what life brings—no sneer

You keep pedaling—great example of work
No cardboard sign for you—corner to lurk

Roberto, your bell has a certain ring charm
Left hand gripped hand bars—no right arm

I paid thrice for the little goodie I bought
No pity from me had you wanted or sought

Right arm was missing from elbow to tip
You touched me today, pal, I'll never yip

I gave you three times what your price was
Couldn't help myself—love ya just because

I turned back to my work—no griping in mind
A message just came by—joy in the grind

Roberto, ring that bell—loud—to be heard
Your message clear, said without a word

⁓ ⁓ ⁓ ⁓ ⁓ ⁓ ⁓ ⁓ ⁓ ⁓ ⁓

Written on occasion of encountering Roberto, the ice cream cart guy. He kept his little business going in spite of missing most of his right arm. He really touched me, and I know I felt a little ashamed of myself for griping about my sore back and arms from raking and shoveling. We go along getting arrogant and prideful and thinking we are something—and along comes someone of very humble means with a great attitude, and we say, "Wow, how can they keep going with their problems and act joyful as well?" Roberto, ring that bell, and if I am in your area again, and I see you, I'll be really glad to buy several things and give you a tip as well. It's not that I have pity on you. It's payback for sharpening my awareness of reality. We leave this scene as I look back and see a small crowd of children buying from Roberto. He is making change using his stubby elbow and his left hand. I stand and watch him pedal into the distance, and I listen to that bell. I ask myself what he does for work when it's cold and wet. Roberto, ring that bell, push those pedals, and thanks for the help.

[Dad, this was beautiful, and you always see the best in others! Thank you for your example of generosity and encouragement to other people, including strangers that bless your path. I love you, Dad, and wouldn't trade you for any other dad in the world. I hope your back and arms aren't too sore. I know how you pour your body and soul into your work, and hopefully, someday soon, you can slow down a bit.

Love, Karen]

⁓ ⁓ ⁓ ⁓ ⁓ ⁓ ⁓ ⁓ ⁓ ⁓ ⁓

Seek My Hide

Seek my hide somewhere in the yard
Keep looking—to find me is hard

Count to twenty and don't look around
After twenty, you can run with a bound

Seeking and hiding is the most fun
When it's darker and there is no sun

A boy chases a girl to the tree
Who gets there first yells—free

The girl runs fast—playing hard to get
Down deep a fire may be lit

Such fun is tops—stars come out
Seek my hide, and I'll shout

No batteries, no monitors, no plugs
Memories of the game have good tugs

Who is it that from the Father doth hide
To really live with him one should abide

He never hides and is easy to find
He'll help you run through the daily grind

My Son ran the race to the tree
My Son was faithful and said you are free

Come out from hiding and show yourself
Or just keep your selfishness on a shelf

Salvation at the tree is free as air
Sins are covered because Jesus was there

You tried to hide your sin from him
Now you know your chances were slim

He knew all along where you were
He sought you with a Holy Spirit stir

Confession and adoption—free from harms
He welcomed you with wide-stretched arms

Written on occasion of remembering all those times of childhood's hide-and-seek games. Early in the game, if you ran fast enough, you could get to the safety tree before the seeker. It was fun when you helped someone else get to the safety tree of freedom too. I wonder how many people are hiding in the darkness and unwilling to run to Jesus. If they only knew they could exchange their position of darkness and lostness for security and freedom, then they too would be running to the freedom tree. Jesus waits for them to declare them safe and free. We leave this scene of children playing hide-and-seek and see them heading back to their homes and winding down for dinner and sleep for a school day tomorrow. The embers of the bonfire and the overcooked marshmallows both lay cooling.

Otoolie

Otoolie, where are you? I need you now
The deadline is near—enter now with a bow

Please come to me—hiding is no longer fun
Got to get things done, and then I have to run

Time is wasting, I need you more than ever
When we are together, you make it clever

You can be replaced, this is what will be
Now I'm frustrated, irritated—please come to me

I've looked for you in crooks and crannies and box
You've let me down even after our talks

Otoolie, you've left me after all we've been through
I wish I knew where you were—haven't a clue

Can't complain about your effective work
I know I've acted so much like a terrible jerk

Your cold shoulder is hard for me to handle
I know I've never walked a mile in your sandal

You'll be replaced, but you'll always be no. 1
I'll never forget our experiences under God's sun

If and when I find you, the past won't matter
We'll carry on just as close as pancake and batter

⌐ ⌐ ⌐ ⌐ ⌐ ⌐ ⌐ ⌐ ⌐ ⌐ ⌐

Written on occasion of having a project and not able to find the right tool, which is the hammer. We had a dinner date with friends, and I was trying to finish up the fence so our dog couldn't get out. We leave this scene as

Otoolie's owner enters the garage half bath and sees Otoolie lying on a shelf. Are we Otoolies for God, or are we unavailable for duty and service? The two men of the foursome trade stories of when they have lost things in the past. The women of the foursome are enjoying chatting about the entrée.

I've Been Here Before

The wind is colder this morning time
Air is smokey and looks like lime

Bills and bills stacked at home
I must go dig in this God's loam

Prayed at hearth then tossed scarf
I'm on the move—soon to haul snarf

I've been here before—state of mind
Help me, Lord, as I nose to the grind

Things are the same—but different day
This is your day, Lord, I pray and pray

I've been here before when I try
Then things seem to go all awry

I've been here before, life is curled
Today it's you and I against this world

People let me down when need is most
Today I'm your guest and you the host

No profit to be found in reject and loss
I lean on you, Lord, you be the great boss

I've been here before, Lord, remember me?
I sidestepped your plan and now on knee

Show me the route—guide this blessed rig
Supply the work, Lord, no job to little or big

I've been here before, Lord, relying on you
Put you to the test in this real-life school

This self-employed contractor needs you
Lord, you can lift a guy and makes things new

You've proven yourself many times over
I need your strength—these weeds aren't clover

Your Word is a lamp unto my feet and legs
Your Word lights my path even in tall dregs

Counting my blessings, but there are too many
I'd be rich if each blessing was only a penny

I've been here before—not knowing what's ahead
I have you, Lord, now, really, why should I dread?

Enemy got up early and greeted me with fear
Back home, wife is praying—what precious dear

If there was no need to lean on you, I'd lose
Trusting and obeying is just what I choose

I love you, Lord, and there's nothing I'd skip
Want to strongly build our eternal relationship

I'm ready to follow you this God-sized day
Lead me to know and do and what to say

This job may lack excitement, surprise, and more
Put this in perspective—it's you that I adore

Through the day, I meet folks that need—uplift
Need to look to you—stop problems that sift

Cherished are the ones who know your purpose
Their relationship with you goes beyond surface

I've been here before, Lord, and today no cringe
Let me touch hem of garment rather than singe

I've been here before Lord when I worried much
Why do I do that when I've experienced your touch?

Read your Word which is my sword—here goes
Enemy is near me, so I must really keep on toes

Enemy is defeated—praise the Lord—oh yes, yes
If you don't know the Savior, your life is guess

Power, purpose, and peace are tools for today
Guilt, shame, fear, loss, hurts—behind me stay

Thank you, Lord, for meeting needs for each mile
My reward for all this—is the light of your smile

⁓　⁓　⁓　⁓　⁓　⁓　⁓　⁓　⁓　⁓　⁓

Written on occasion of not having a lot of desire to work today. Sometimes I complain about my work when others would be happy to have a job. It's up to the Lord how much money I make. It's more important if I am living for Him and make decisions with eternal values in view.

Proverbs 3:5, 6 are a loving commandment with concrete promise indeed. May I plant today, Lord, and may there be a harvest of that seed.

⁓　⁓　⁓　⁓　⁓　⁓　⁓　⁓　⁓　⁓　⁓

Little Cabin

We hiked for hours and arrived
The scene beautiful not contrived

Water bucket hung on rusty nail
Crossing the porch was a snail

Years now since there was life
Up here is an absence of strife

Hinges groaned as door swung
There was a ladder-missing rung

Cookstove's good and wood nearby
My imagination pulled out a pie

Eve was cool so lit some heat
Absolutely nothing was very neat

Little cabin, you are so dear to me
Here life is free and knows no fee

No TV and no bothering tele calls
Sit and drink coffee and hear squalls

No broken glass in the window rill
A few tools were in a box—a drill

Sun's going down—better pick spot
Time for some split pea I brought

The thin tarp now went down first
Spiders out seen a lot—isn't worst

Guard me with rifle—privy I come
If mountain lion jumps, rifle, not mum

We saw bear tracks, this I know
After our visit there, face can show

Memories flood us like sunami waves
Tonight you are the princess, I the nave

Door is bolted and now the fire is out
No tub here and no drip from a spout

Hear something scratching on outside
Probably a raccoon wanting in to abide

One night here gives enough to last
Next year again, we'll relive the past

So many memories, but one is pure bliss
Here is where I received your first kiss

Married now and doing this or that
Your love will never become old hat

Hold me close and in morning just stare
If in the only window, you see a bear

Little cabin you are quite an adventure
If I am scared, I'll bite hard on my denture

Little cabin of memories, tonight I am beat
Wouldn't pass this up—our special retreat

Good night, angel, joy of my busy life
Imagine soft marchers and one playing fife

Oh Lord, of tender mercies meet our need
Help us always to avoid anger and greed

May we always thirst for righteousness
May we live by faith and not try to guess

Little cabin tomorrow, we'll leave here
We'll try to come back in about a year

Our true love is carved on the pine tree
Hearts will change—deepen in love, you see

I'm glad we hiked and couldn't have drove
I always remember that pop-belly stove

This place is filled with joy and much charm
Whoops—almost asked you—to turn on alarm

Written on occasion of going back in time to a special place that is partly imaginary, but the fact of love is totally real and true. We all need to step back for a while and retreat to a safe place where we are not interrupted by the "things of this world." Be still and know that God is God. You might like to know that when mee lady went out in the morning, a momma bear and cubs could be seen going behind a distant boulder. Dee, protector, stood guard until mee lady returned to carry her backpack. After pictures and a long kiss, they continued climbing to the upper lake, and the rest of the family was happy to see them. The little cabin now sleeps while the spiders and raccoons make their way to center stage. Back at the lake, lil' J.T. runs up to his grandma and asks her how she liked roughing it. Super—as she held her protector's hand, and in case you were wondering, no shots were fired. I love you so much, Grandma and Papa.

The Wonder of This Children's Land

Whatever age, there is a kid in me
So much to do and so much to see

This is a place to brag about
Teakettle even has a big spout

Place was built with hammer and crane
Do you know that guy named Shane

Guy named Shane, ideas up his sleeve
So much was done by sidekick Steve

At first, it seemed like such a mess
Along came somebody named Hess

Use your eyes and take a full scan
Ness really knew the full plan

Who is that guy that worked thru lunch?
His work has a touch of air e donch

Who could tally the hours on hours
Forward march—let naysayers be in sours

Yes, little kid, say it, "Please, please do"
I love it, I love it, and a giant, big thank-you

Old park closed, new park ideas soared
Really love the people on the board

The wonder of this place is so evident
An hour here will seem like a minute spent

Wriggle and giggle and enjoy being here
GVRD says to each child, "We love you dear"

〜 〜 〜 〜 〜 〜 〜 〜 〜 〜 〜

Written on occasion of being grateful for the opportunity to help develop Children's Wonderland managed by the Greater Vallejo Recreation District. My company did a fair amount of work here, and I enjoyed doing it. One day in Vietnam, I asked God to get me out of there alive, and I would serve him by serving young people. Well, this is what I try to do and am thankful to the leadership of GVRD for allowing me to have a part in all this. Tonight, I chose to be with my loving grandchildren out of town. But really, am sorry I couldn't attend the dedication of the park. I just know there was a lot of cheerfulness in the crowd. My reward will be when I can walk hand in hand with my grandchildren through the castle and into the wonder of this—children's land.

〜 〜 〜 〜 〜 〜 〜 〜 〜 〜 〜

Countertops

Careful not to damage the surface
Things are placed with soft grace

Granite gives a deep shine and glow
Past countertops cleaning was slow

No cracks or pitted areas to grime
Hard to realize these are really mine

No toys, tools, or high-heel shoes
These a time-out will be a choose

Items glide on the surface without grout
So happy now, I could just about shout

Looking back, I remember tops of wood
Tops of Formica and tile and tops of mood

Swishing them clean as if in a dance
These counters get a second glance

No paint, no glue, no tightening needed
Joints nearly invisible, contractor creeded

Cups and saucers and vases sound special
Items fit flat without any wrestle

Somewhere in a quarry, these stones were large
Hewn from God's creation and sent by barge

Slabbed and polished to a wet-look pleasing
Formica and tile now can give a quising

Look so nice, they almost say good morning
Thanks, Lord, they are so adoring

I sit on a stool at the breakfast counter
The granite pattern and color—I'm no pouter

Widths and lengths and starts and stops
These flat surfaces are countertops

Written on occasion of Jordan and Karen moving into their new custom home.

Trumpeter's Counseling

The sound can be mellow and soft
It can be low or at times be aloft

It's sound can seem like a voice
Jazz, blues, march, your choice

One end is the mouthpiece, other the bell
Air-and-mouth-pressure sound will tell

Push valve down and sounds goes round
Every player has a favorite sound

Sound the call forward to battle
If only the enemy would skedaddle

The other sound is not really neat
It means unprepared and now a retreat

Taps played under sky of sun or gray
Won't forget or from love stray

Back then, daily practice seemed a bore
Now for pleasure, I'll just play more

Discipline and passion rolled into one
Trumpeter's sound is never done

Mouth muscles and tight lips, I confess
Should make a trumpeter learn a kiss

Session now over and did hit every note
Trumpet in case and slip on my coat

Brisk air, and I walk tall and stout
A good trumpeter could have clout

Trumpet sounds happy lots of times
Cases lie open for nickels and dimes

Heralding crisp and in three parts
Notes sound like vocal darts

Trumpet will sound, and time will pause
Christ will be exalted because he draws

The saved gather on the other shore
Up yonder roll is called "enter this door"

Lord, my trumpet, I give to thee
Make notes sound heavenly

When I play, I will not tire
Hopefully, a younger to inspire

Don't neglect it or from it stray
Faithfully play it, or get out of way

Someone will enjoy plain note or trill
Rejecting your trumpet hurts a skill

So play now with passion to use
Your sound will never be called refuse

Sort of like you, Lord, the breath you give
Gives me the desire for you to live

The trumpeter breathes into tubular device
Shatters ears or sounds really, really nice

Help me, Lord, with each and every part
Don't breathe from lungs, but from your heart

~ ~ ~ ~ ~ ~ ~ ~ ~ ~ ~

Written on occasion of enjoying the trumpet and thankful it is a lifetime skill.
Written as a tribute to beloved brothers Jon and Bill who played trumpet-
and to Mom and Dad and Klaris and Connie who endured the listening.

~ ~ ~ ~ ~ ~ ~ ~ ~ ~

Enjoy Kidding Around

We came home on the bus
My dad said, "Run—be in a rush"

To the barn we ran
A matter of life or death

There were two newborns
Five minutes old

So full of life
This story must be told

Wish the momma goat waited
Till the human kids got home

Wanted her to wait till you arrived
Two little kid's goats 100 percent survived

Myrtle's momma was so proud
Breathing back to norm

Lil' barn full now a shroud
Scene was such a dorm

Human kids meet goat kids
Approval came through tall

Lively tenants paid no rent
Blessed ones wer' heav'sent

Written on occasion of seeing and knowing the joy and excitement on my children's faces when they first saw the baby goats. A memory I'll never forget.

100 Percent = 0.25

Yes, it is true
The rule is to accrue

To reach the quarter
Takes more than mortar

Some look to the full one
Others see it as a sum

A quarter plus three equals a whole
Can't go ahead while on the dole

Aspire and perspire the whole to reach
Hard work and dedication know no breach

One quarter is now a goal won
This paramed is our dear son

Leading at one quarter is a toll
Leaders say let's roll

Prepared and confident from yesterday
Code threes mean I'll always pray

Stand on one quarter and look out there
Yes, this paramed can say I really care

Papers and needles and gurneys bring strife
I'm helping someone to maintain life

Lord, I need your strength to make it through
All the responsibility gives me a lot to do

Three quarters more, I'll survive
Don't break my stride with your jive

One lap down, three to go
I'll respond even in the snow

Three quarters more and no lackluster
To succeed, follow just one master

My eyes droop, and I'm ready for bed
Tomorrow, I need to know just what med

Cheer me on, cheer me on with steady voice
Three quarters more, then eye can be moist

The banner of God's love flies in front of me
I claim promises, obedience and think triumphantly

Second quarter comes tomorrow, you see
One quarter plus, that's what it'll be

More than a starter and not finished yet
My face and heart to the cold wind I'll set

One quarter of blessings, I've already counted
The horse of perseverance, I've just mounted

Pressures come down as if out of a funnel
God says, "There is light at the end of the tunnel"

Good night to it all, I'll now let it rest
Tomorrow with help of the Lord, I'll do my best

Written on occasion of thinking about goals and aspirations and working hard.

Door of Opportunity

The walk was not too long
Sometimes I heard a song

I didn't know above me
God had a bird singing

Sometimes the bird I didn't see
However, melodies were ringing

The door had two sides
Couldn't wait to see the other

This side was to enter
Other was an adventure

Some doors I cannot open
God has something better

Doors that are unlocked
Announced in a letter

Some doors are faithful and true
Don't mean to take for granted

Glad some doors are locked
Label on them is "return back"

I run from those doors now
Forward to adventure, I plow

One door I search for every day
Very difficult to find

Door marked "God's wisdom"
Has a number near the top

Easiest number under the son
You see, its no. 1

First door, it is clear
All the others follow near

Now I see wisdom, joy, and peace
Love for others will increase

Look over there see that door of bold
C means confidence, many have told

Pressures come with a crush
God's voice comes in a hush

One door is always unlocked
No matter if life is bright or gray

Door leads to nothing of shock
It's the door labeled Pray

No map to these doors is needed
His voice is to be heeded

The adventurous can understand
Be willing to take Him by the hand

     ~   ~   ~   ~   ~   ~   ~   ~   ~   ~   ~

Written on occasion of remembering the little study building we prepared for
this journey of study into becoming a paramedic. For son Jon from Dad.

     ~   ~   ~   ~   ~   ~   ~   ~   ~   ~   ~

THOMAS A. NORDSTROM

Report

The main nain in Spain was huge
The name on the side said puge

Great ride on this big iron horse
I pretended I was the engineer of course

The power, the rumble, the speed, and the roar
It was exciting—bring on more

As we made a turn on the strong steel track
A little boy waved from a small wooden shack

The falling snow made the view a little vague
But I did see he was missing part of a leg

Something inside of me made me pray
His smile from my mind will never stray

At the station, the engineer was walking near
Children were running around with cheer

Loudly, I said can I speak to you, sir
Yes, my lad, I'll listen and not stir

Do you know the little boy that lives a little back
The boy in the little wooden shack?

Oh yes, my lad, he is my son
There was a time when he could run

A black bear attacked us two years ago
It knocked us down on the ground so low

My son hobbled to the gun nearer to him than I
He heard his mother as she gave a loud cry

The bullet and the bear, yes, they did meet
The bear roared in pain and made a retreat

He's a hero to everyone that knows
On his face, the joy glows

The shack is so little, how do you live?
At peace with each other, no sifter or sieve

The house is still ours, but we moved out
Just then the boy heard a big shout

All aboard was the conductor's command
No time for any playing in dirt or in sand

We now live in a big house in town farther up
We thank the Lord as we talk and sup

Here, sir, for your son, I want to give this
This little nain will add to his Christmas bliss

He stops at the shack every day for an hour
He loves me so much, and when he waves, there is power

Mom, Dad, and I were together, you see
Your son will be blessed by God at the tree

The engineer waved and hurried to the engine back
Cars jolted forward as they moved down the track

I'm resting now, and it's half past seven
That nain blessing was engineered in heaven

⌐ ⌐ ⌐ ⌐ ⌐ ⌐ ⌐ ⌐ ⌐ ⌐ ⌐

Written on occasion of thinking about Logan and a story about an engineer
who has a little boy and how life's realities unfold sometimes. Written for Logan
to read later on and to know that blessing others is always part of God's will.

⌐ ⌐ ⌐ ⌐ ⌐ ⌐ ⌐ ⌐ ⌐ ⌐ ⌐

Is That Guy Pewless?

Hello Chris from Tom from Nam
Taking a break from lam and jam

Bobbi and I will travel short way
We'll be back from a brief stay

Bobbi's birthday weekend break
Breathing room for to take

Sunday, we'll worship for sure
Time flies and what a blur

We'll miss you guys and dolls
Every day a new charm enthralls

Garret, Kennedy, and Gage, sit over there
Momma Lisa's eyes show guidance and care

Daddy Chris gives everyone a gift
Spiritual truths and facts to lift

We'll be there in heart and mind
Bodies will other places find

Tom will be back for the six o'clock serv
He'll safely travel the line and curve

Holy Spirit, help them to again give the best
Building together here at Your hillcrest

This spiritual clinic sees transformation oft
The lighthouse light will never be quaffed

Thanks for all you do and more
Don't ever lose your love for Him to adore

Lord, build a fire under folks with Your flame
Make them break the habit of pointing to blame

In Your house, we sing and never ever chant
Two-edged sword performs a heart transplant

We'll be back our steps to retrace
We'll sit and be showing our joyfulness face

Counting my blessings and so much to see
Eternity with the offspring Cowan three

Make my life a message board for You
May others read humbleness too

～　～　～　～　～　～　～　～　～　～　～

Written on occasion of our leaving for a birthday weekend for Bobbi. Thanks, Lord, that when we return, you will be there as usual with a flame to burn.

～　～　～　～　～　～　～　～　～　～　～

The Worm is Already There

When on a quick stroll, I fell
Resultant pain was not swell

Soon I gathered my bones and flesh
No doubt about it, not even a guess

Hurting and spurting inside, I crept
This lesson learned to its depth

This was cross walking with a 'tude
Taking on now a much different mood

When on the ground, a worm I could stare
Yes, because it was already there

⌐   ⌐   ⌐   ⌐   ⌐   ⌐   ⌐   ⌐   ⌐   ⌐   ⌐

Written on occasion of being in a hurry and kicking something out of the way, causing me to sprain my ankle.

⌐   ⌐   ⌐   ⌐   ⌐   ⌐   ⌐   ⌐   ⌐   ⌐   ⌐

Less of Self or Selfless

What happened to the volume and bustle?
This house is too quiet, no kid fussel

Is it less of self or selfless with joy?
I interact with children and a toy

Grandchildren often do the opposite
Grandpa instructs on safety—no quit

Less of self is when you lose stress
She twirls in her boot-e-fol dress

Is it truly selfless when they share?
I learn to referee when Pop's a snare

Grandpa knows from just one clue
Snare happens when nap is due

Thank-you's and say yes please
Selfless words put us at ease

~ ~ ~ ~ ~ ~ ~ ~ ~ ~ ~

Written on occasion of knowing when one or more of my angels needs a nap. Grandpa also needs a nap—sometimes called a break.

~ ~ ~ ~ ~ ~ ~ ~ ~ ~ ~

Surfaces of Flat

Metal shelves might have rust
Most shelves have some dust

Flat surfaces can get clutter
Neat freak might just mutter

That stuff is only temporary pile
Relax, don't get into a big rile

Flat surfaces cleaned—now guests
No clutter can be seen—only best

Flat surface, clear of stuff—odd
Quickly, add a paper, book, or clod

When I lose something, soon find
It was right there, was I blind?

None of my surfaces do I adore
'Tis better the stuff is off the floor

There's one surface that releases hoard
"Must move on," says the ironing board

Medicine cabinet surfaces only four
Guests! Find what you're looking for

One shelf is a getter of respect
It is full of family pics and so decked

Over there is a surface so reliable
I sit there and cherish the family Bible

Written on occasion of remembering how fast I can put something on a surface that is available. Some picture-hanging tools and supplies have been near the back of my darling wife's dresser for several months. They are out of view, and what can I say, the surface was there, and I made it a victim of my ability to lie things around. Sometimes I look for one thing I have misplaced and wind up finding something else I was looking for and had given up ever finding. I feel sorry for all you neat freaks out there in the dust-free environment. I challenge you to leave something lying around even for a few minutes. Should you need the courage or training on how to live a more relaxed style, come on over but call first. I may be in the middle of trying to find something. Excuse me now. It's time for me to look for something that will change my life. I know right where it is though, and you can join me with tea or coffee as we look and discover God's truths in his Word that is lying on the flat surface. Love, a partially trained husband.

For Eyes

The blur was giving me a headache
I couldn't see the path to take

Was there a cliff over there?
The blur caused me to stare

I stumbled on a rock at the edge
Hoped for something like a hedge

The blur darkened as I groped
I crawled as I cried and coped

My foot now felt the cliff's edge
I lay motionless on this little ledge

Updraft winds from the valley below
Proved again that nature was a foe

Rain soaked me down to the bone
Fear of death on my face now shown

Loose rocks fell off the craggy stage
Seconds later, they landed in the crage

I slid in the mud, and both feet were over
Lightning strikes made me so very sober

Lying motionless, I wondered my fate
Was today going to be my ending date?

Wind and rain pounded me even harder
Yelled help so loud to stretch a garter

This crisis time left me empty of my self
I cried dear Lord get me off this shelf

Slipping more now my knees are there
Slowly sliding out to the thin air

I slid some more with nothing to grip
Wasted now as a tea bag not to drip

The valley floor must be a thousand feet
Would I land on my head or on my seat?

Futilely, I tried to grip the mud with my nails
Life flashed before me as if on fast sails

Sliding now over edge to my certain doom
It wasn't crowded there—was lots of room

I yelled noooooooooooo all the way down
Soon I would be wearing a heavenly gown

Falling to my death, and then I'd be mute
Oh God, please send me a blessed parachute

The updrafts were strong and slowed me
I fell in soft marsh near tall heather swee

My fall was cushioned by tangled growth
Gained consciousness later with a poath

This small area only a few feet across
All by itself in this floor of rocky dross

Had I landed elsewhere that horrific night
No hope to survive hitting the rocky blight

Learned my lesson and now no push by self
The Bible is my companion—no longer on shelf

God let me fall the reason is now known
He wanted the credit and power to be shown

I try hard now to avoid any danger zone
I don't want to be unprotected and alone

Sometimes it takes near death to understand
So sweet to trust in Jesus in hollow of His hand

⁓   ⁓   ⁓   ⁓   ⁓   ⁓   ⁓   ⁓   ⁓   ⁓   ⁓

Written on occasion of thinking about the times that I really messed up, and
the good Lord saw me through it and kept me from being destroyed on the
rocks of hard knocks. This is a lesson that people go through several times
in their life. Trusting and obeying can prevent a lot of stress.

⁓   ⁓   ⁓   ⁓   ⁓   ⁓   ⁓   ⁓   ⁓   ⁓   ⁓

Can Do

Little bird I gave you that name
It was because your leg was lame

You had the work ethic strong
You even demonstrated a song

I always was happy to see you
You were my pal but had no clue

I would have tried to feed you worms
You would eat even all the germs

I projected out to you, lil' friend
A message of working to the end

I'm not lame but am self-employed
Looking out for dangers I am coyed

That lame leg never slowed you
You were purpose driven and true

We all have dangers every day
Stray cats wanted you to stay

Haven't seen you for a long while
One of those cats gave you a smile

A cat one day had a bird in clutch
My heart sank this was too much

It must have been you—no return
You showed me lessons to learn

Don't get lazy—the enemy will pounce
Be vigilant and have a snappy bounce

Keep going hard and don't blame God
Just when you need, he'll prize the sod

A juicy worm awaits your deep search
Insects will be in the bark of birch

You inspired me, pal, with your pep
The lurking enemy showed guile rep

Thanks for being a winged cheer
I loved it when you were so near

Bye, my hero of life's battles fought
I learned the lessons that you taught

Written on occasion of thinking back on those mornings when Can Do would be in the yard, working away at gathering with seemingly no concern that he had to lean over to peck for food. If he could have talked, he might have said, Thanks for putting out the bird food—sure makes it easier to take food back to the nest." I don't think about my injured leg anymore. I just figure it's not important compared to thinking about how to avoid getting eaten alive by those cats that cruise through here. Mom needs my help since Dad got caught by two cats from different directions. Remember, don't let too much of yesterday use up too much of today. "See ya later," I hear mom calling.

Cactus Cuties

Cactus Cuties came to me on the Internet
Their singing "I'll Never Ever Forget"

They sing the national anthem from hearts
This VN vet was blessed with special marks

I listen and relisten—can't get enough
Being a Vietnam vet at times is quite rough

Cactus Cuties, you are so true and American
I hope you will find out—I'm a very big fan

My mind and soul were on the chopping block
I got older there—no speeding of clock

You've helped me come closer to back home
I try to forget bad memories—like a comb

Your singing is so perfect—to bless
Thank you, thank you—love, I confess

Millions have been touched by your love
When you sing, I imagine a peaceful dove

You give us what's good about the USA
When you sing, I close my eyes and pray

Pray for me—emotionally coming home
Your singing is like diamonds on chrome

You prove that his stars are still there
Thank you for your pride of country dear

Thank you all four for loving we vets
You've brought me closer with no regrets

I love to sing, and I sing along with you
Don't ever forget this fan is true blue

God bless you for what you represent
From God, your talent has been lent

One thing I carry in my backpack of duties
An uplifting time hearing the Cactus Cuties

~   ~   ~   ~   ~   ~   ~   ~   ~   ~   ~

Written on occasion of falling in love again with everything bright and beautiful and special about the good ole USA. These four girls have touched my soul, and God knows I needed it. PTSD is a debilitating condition. I am leaning on the Savior Jesus Christ to lift me above the negative.

I want to put new words to the PTSD, and it is "past thoughts surreally dwell." I've heard you voice, your thanks for the heritage left by those who gave their service, and others who gave their service and their life. If Thomas Kinkaide was asked to paint a picture of patriotism—it would be a picture of the cactus cuties performing. Thank you for your service to our great country, and God bless you richly. From Vietnam vet Tom.

~   ~   ~   ~   ~   ~   ~   ~   ~   ~   ~

I Will and I Do

Things were tough the first year
Trailer was short from hitch to rear

We were married now for keeps
Honey, you tell me your heart leaps

We long for a bigger place and space
We hate debt, and that is our case

No one would visit us—place small
No credit cards for us—cash crawl

We financially crawled but joy filled
Our savings grew, and hopes thrilled

We agreed on this before, I said I do
Financial woes meant so much boohoo

I was pregnant and not working a job
Darling didn't want money—this to rob

Both our cars were paid for but old
We were out of debt and not a scold

Our savings grew and so did the baby
Paid cash for a little house—a heyday

Parked that old trailer in the back
Home was awesome—cake on rack

Darling worked so hard—even late
He was promoted—proud of my mate

Our church announced seminar on money
We have no problems, thanks, honey

A new friend said you are so happy
I am but some days don't feel snappy

New friend said, so much in debt
Being married is becoming a regret

Everything paid for and money in bank
Willpower working but God to thank

Our church has a money seminar
Helps people into reality with a jar

With God, all things are possible, dear
We are not perfect but debt is clear

Did without but knew where we were going
All of this time, our savings were growing

Turned down credit cards one by one
We paid cash and was really, really fun

We always give God tithe and get blessed
We still have money and aren't stressed

Spend my time getting ready for our child
Some people show off and spending is wild

We eat well and do fun weekend trips
Pulling our old trailer gives happy lips

I have the freedom to- buy what I want
Would rather save than have heart gaunt

Aren't afraid to use secondhand things
Some things are great even with dings

Listen, friend, here is what I've learned
Staying out of debt is happiness earned

I will and I do mean stay true and blue
Don't be ruled by things, let God rule

Don't see a sale and into the store dash
Buy just what you need and pay cash

~   ~   ~   ~   ~   ~   ~   ~   ~   ~   ~

Written on occasion of thinking about the clean feeling after paying something off. Debts are like masters, and we therefore are the slaves. Money stress has ruined many marriages. Hey, don't worry about what the neighbors think of you. More importantly is what you think of yourself and what you are doing for Christ. Oh, did I tell you our church is having a seminar on money and financial responsible living? Would you excuse me? My darling is coming home, and after dinner, we are picking out baby furniture. Another day is almost through and more in the bank did accrue. Tomorrow, we pay cash for the baby furniture. Thank you. We leave this scene with the couple at the store and the clerk says, "Charge or cash?" My darling says, "Cash?"

~   ~   ~   ~   ~   ~   ~   ~   ~   ~   ~